SCHOLASTIC

M000306672

EARLY LEARNING

READY TO LEARN

Alphabet • Numbers • Colors • Shapes • Patterns

New York • Toronto • London • Auckland • Sydney
Mexico City • New Delhi • Hong Kong • Buenos Aires

Cover design: Tannaz Fassihi; Cover illustration: Jason Dove
Interior design: Michelle H. Kim
Interior illustration: Doug Jones

ISBN: 978-1-338-32316-0
Copyright © 2018 by Scholastic Inc.
All rights reserved.
Printed in the U.S.A.
First printing, September 2018.

4 5 6 7 8 9 10   02   24 23 22 21 20 19

Contents

Dear Parent,

Thanks for choosing this workbook! For nearly a century, Scholastic has been a trusted leader in educational publishing. We firmly believe that it is never too early to begin the learning journey, especially when that journey includes delightful skill-building activities that are just right for young children.

On the pages that follow, you'll find hundreds of playful activities that are designed to keep your child engaged and challenged, but not overwhelmed. The book is organized into 30 sets, with each set focusing on a particular skill. (Turn the page for a list of skills.) Each set provides repeated practice to help your child gain confidence as he or she masters the skill.

Inside this book, you'll also find:

- ★ A handy chart at the beginning of each set to track your child's progress

- ★ 100+ colorful stickers (Helpful hint: Use these as rewards for completing each set.)

- ★ Ideas for fun family activities you can do with your child

- ★ A certificate of achievement to celebrate your child's accomplishments

The time is right to start your child on the path to a lifetime of learning success!

Sincerely,

The editors

Let's Get Ready to Learn!

This activity book has been carefully designed to help ensure that your child has the tools he or she needs to excel in school. The formatted activities invite your child to identify, trace, match, graph, classify, and more! Your child will gain lots of experience with the target skill, helping to set the stage for excitement and confidence in learning.

On the 200-plus pages that follow, your child will:

ALPHABET

- ★ Trace and write letters of the alphabet
- ★ Identify the missing letter in a sequence of letters
- ★ Recognize uppercase and lowercase letters
- ★ Match uppercase letters to lowercase letters
- ★ Graph uppercase and lowercase letters
- ★ Identify words that begin with each letter sound

NUMBERS

- ★ Trace and write numbers 1 to 100 and number words
- ★ Count from 1 to 100
- ★ Fill in missing numbers in a sequence of numbers
- ★ Use number lines
- ★ Match numbers to quantities
- ★ Add one or ten more to a number

BASIC CONCEPTS

- ★ Identify and trace shapes and colors
- ★ Recognize colors
- ★ Trace color and shape words
- ★ Match real life objects to their color or shape
- ★ Count objects and graph the number of objects in a category
- ★ Identify the next object in a pattern
- ★ Recognize items that are alike or different in a group
- ★ Classify and sequence objects
- ★ Compare objects
- ★ Complete color-by-shape pictures

Early Learning: Ready to Learn is filled with motivating, special features including:

A handy chart at the start of each set that lets your child track his or her progress

Engaging activities that make learning fun

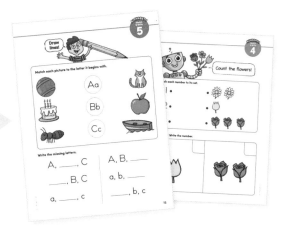

A review page that reinforces the target skill and can be used to assess your child's learning

Fun motivating stickers to celebrate your child's milestones

A certificate of achievement to reward your child's accomplishments

Tips for Using This Book

★ **Pick a good time** for your child to work. You may want to do it around mid-morning after play or early afternoon when your child is not too tired.

★ **Make sure your child has all the supplies** he or she needs, such as pencils and an eraser. Designate a special place for your child to work.

★ **Encourage your child to complete activities, but don't force the issue.** While you may want to ensure that your child succeeds, it's also important that he or she maintains a positive and relaxed attitude toward learning.

★ **Celebrate your child's accomplishments** by letting him or her affix stickers to completed sets of activities.

★ **Determine if your child needs help** completing the activity pages by giving him or her a few moments to review the page he or she will be working on. Then ask your child to describe what he or she will be doing on the pages. If your child needs support, try offering a choice about which family member might help. Giving your child a choice can help boost confidence and help him or her feel more ownership of the work to be done.

★ **Present your child with the certificate of achievement** on page 255 when he or she has completed the activity book. Feel free to frame or laminate the certificate and display it on the wall for everyone to see. Your child will be so proud!

ALPHABET

Family Activities

Here are some skill-building activities that you and your child might enjoy.

ABC Order

Read a list of five to seven words to your child, such as the days of the week or the ingredients for a tasty sandwich. Then have him or her put the words in alphabetical order.

Letter Squares

Write each letter of your child's name (first and/or last) on a small square sheet of paper, then put the pieces inside an envelope. Give the letters to your child and have him or her use the letters to create different words.

Find the Letter

While reading the newspaper or a magazine, encourage your child to look for words that begin with the same letter as his or her name. Read the words together aloud. Then, ask your child to think of as many words as possible that begin with the same letter.

Magic Letters

Buy a set of magnetic letters so your child can form words on the refrigerator while you cook.

Trace each letter.

LETTERS
A B C

Hi!

Color in each box when you complete the activity.

1 Introduction	**2** Aa	**3** Bb	**4** Cc
5 Match & Write	**6** Color & Match	**7** Graph	**8** Review

© Scholastic Inc.

11

Trace, then write.

Color each picture that begins with the A sound.

Circle each A and a.

A N A q a

a b A g W

Apple!

Draw lines!

Match each picture to the letter it begins with.

Write the missing letters.

A, _____, C   A, B, _____

_____, B, C   a, b, _____

a, _____, c   _____, b, c

A= red   B= blue   C= brown

Use the code to color the picture.

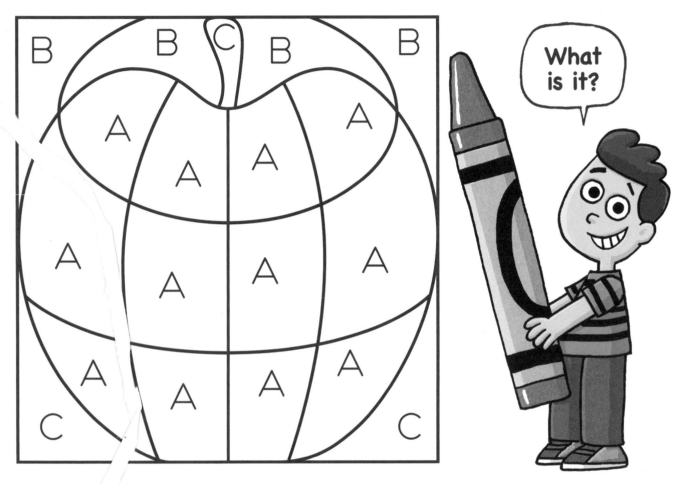

What is it?

Match the letters.

C •   • a
B •   • c
A •   • b

A •   • c
C •   • b
B •   • a

Count and graph the letters.

b C c
B b B
A A
B C
C B
B
A a c

Say each letter!

	A	a	B	b	C	c
4						
3						
2						
1						

Great work! Bye!

Fill in the letters. Color the pictures.

 A
B
C

_____ is for  .

_____ is for  .

_____ is for  .

Write the first letter for each word.

a
b
c

_____up

_____pple

_____ed

Trace each letter.

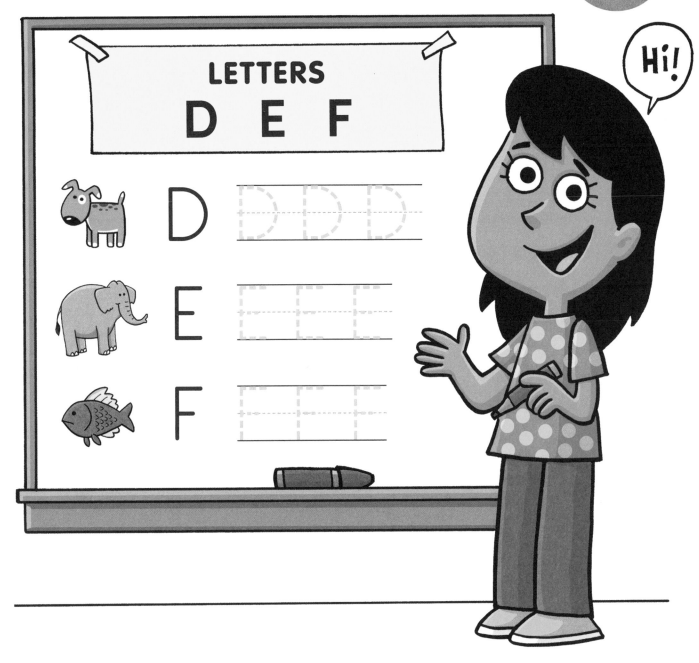

Color in each box when you complete the activity.

1 Introduction	2 Dd	3 Ee	4 Ff
5 Match & Write	6 Color & Match	7 Graph	8 Review

Trace, then write.

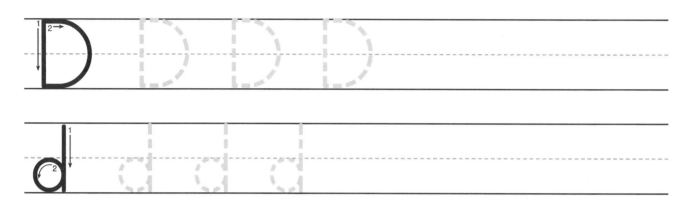

Color each picture that begins with the D sound.

Circle each D and d.

d	p	P	D	Q
D	d	D	b	d

Dinosaur!

Trace, then write.

e e e e

Color each picture that begins with the E sound.

Circle each E and e.

E F e E c

R R e r E e

Elf!

Trace, then write.

Color each picture that begins with the F sound.

Circle each F and f.

f	t	f	F	f
I	F	E	R	F

Feather!

Draw lines!

Match each picture to the letter it begins with.

Dd

Ee

Ff

Write the missing letters.

D, E, _____   _____, E, F

d, _____, f   D, _____, F

d, e, _____   _____, e, f

 D= yellow   E= green   F= blue

Use the code to color the picture.

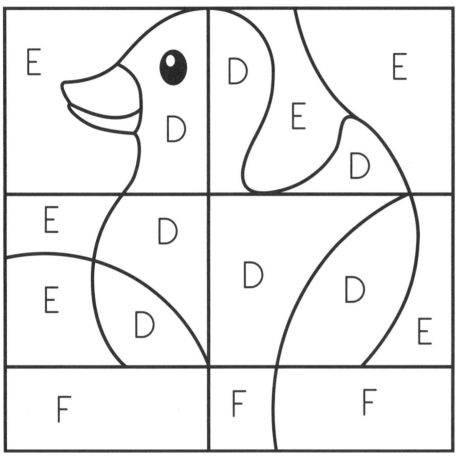

What
is it?

Match the letters.

E •   • f   D •   • f

D •   • e   F •   • d

F •   • d   E •   • e

Count and graph the letters.

d f e
d D
D E D
F E
f
D f
d F

Say each
letter!

	D	d	E	e	F	f
4						
3						
2						
1						

Fill in the letters. Color the pictures.

D
E
F

_____ is for  .

_____ is for .

_____ is for  .

Write the first letter for each word.

d
e
f

 _____og

 _____ish

_____lf

Trace each letter.

Color in each box when you complete the activity.

1	2	3	4
Introduction	Gg	Hh	Ii
5	**6**	**7**	**8**
Match & Write	Color & Match	Graph	Review

Trace, then write.

G G G G

g g g g

Color each picture that begins with the G sound.

Circle each G and g.

C   g   G   q   G

p   D   g   G   g

Gift!

Trace, then write.

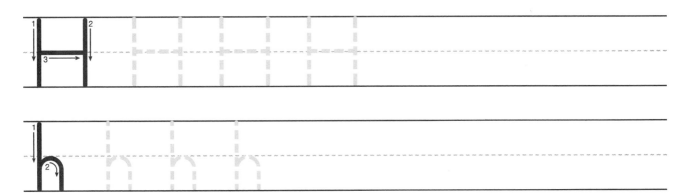

Color each picture that begins with the H sound.

Circle each H and h.

H	k	b	h	H
T	h	H	K	h

Hat!

Trace, then write.

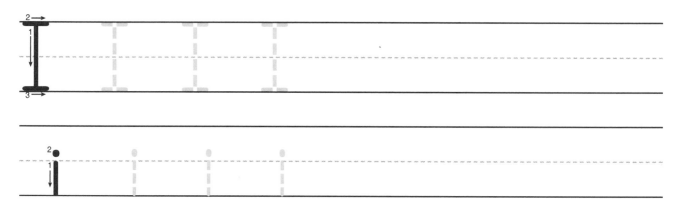

Color each picture that begins with the I sound.

Circle each I and i.

i	J	j	T	i
I	T	I	i	I

Invitation!

Draw lines!

Match each picture to the letter it begins with.

Gg

Hh

Ii

Write the missing letters.

G, _____, I   _____, H, I

G, H, _____   g, h, _____

g, _____, i   _____, h, i

G=  brown   H= blue   I= yellow

Use the code to color the picture.

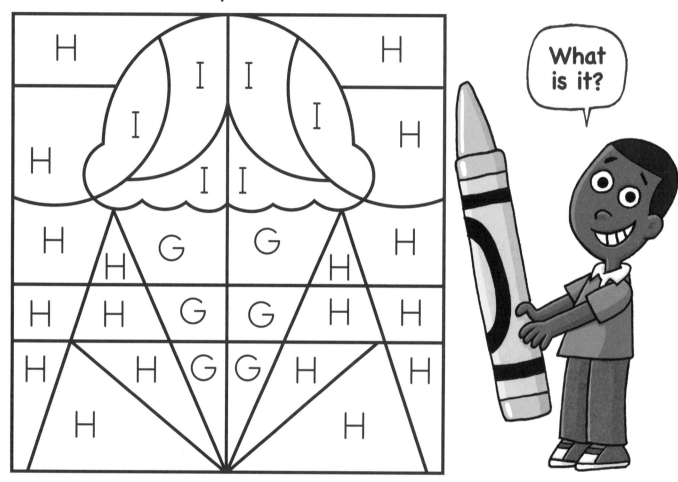

What is it?

Match the letters.

H •	• i		I •	• h
I •	• g		G •	• i
G •	• h		H •	• g

Count and graph the letters.

Say each
letter!

g I i

G H h H

G

H I

I h H

H g h

	G	g	H	h	I	i
4						
3						
2						
1						

Great work! Bye!

Fill in the letters. Color the pictures.

G H I

_____ is for  .

_____ is for  .

_____ is for  .

Write the first letter for each word.

g h i

   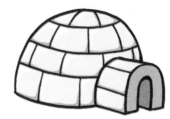   

____en   ____gloo   ____oat

34

Trace each letter.

LETTERS
J K L

J

K

L

Hi!

Color in each box when you complete the activity.

1 Introduction	**2** Jj	**3** Kk	**4** Ll
5 Match & Write	**6** Color & Match	**7** Graph	**8** Review

Trace, then write.

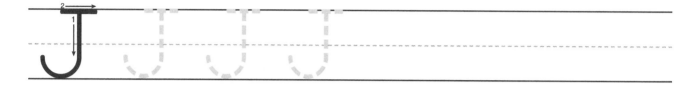

Color each picture that begins with the J sound.

Circle each J and j.

J	I	j	J	J
j	i	T	t	j

Juggle!

Trace, then write.

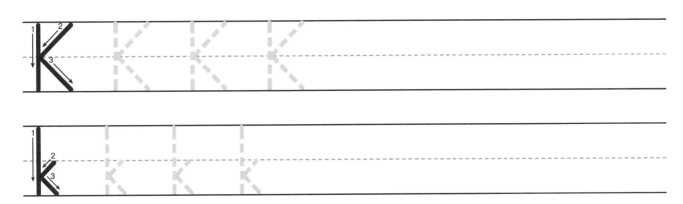

Color each picture that begins with the K sound.

Circle each K and k.

K   k   T   K   K

k   h   R   k   f

Key!

Trace, then write.

Color each picture that begins with the L sound.

Circle each L and l.

t L T L I

L I f E I

Ladybug!

Draw lines!

Match each picture to the letter it begins with.

Jj

Kk

Ll

JUICE

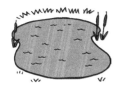

Write the missing letters.

_____ , K, L

j, _____ , l

J, K, _____

j, k, _____

J, _____ , L

_____ , k, l

J =  blue K = yellow L = purple

Use the code to color the picture.

Match the letters.

L •   • l   J •   • k

J •   • k   L •   • j

K •   • j   K •   • l

What
is it?

40

Count and graph the letters.

Say each letter!

	J	j	K	k	L	l
4						
3						
2						
1						

Great work! Bye!

Fill in the letters. Color the pictures.

J
K
L

_____ is for  .

_____ is for  .

_____ is for  .

Write the first letter for each word.

j
k
l

 _____ing

 _____eaf

 _____et

Trace each letter.

LETTERS
M N O

Hi!

Color in each box when you complete the activity.

1	2	3	4
Introduction	Mm	Nn	Oo
5	**6**	**7**	**8**
Match & Write	Color & Match	Graph	Review

Trace, then write.

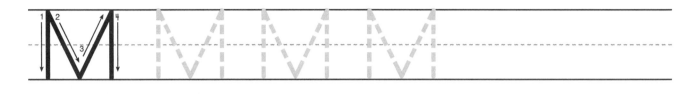

M

m

Color each picture that begins with the M sound.

Circle each M and m.

M   m   W   h   M

m   n   M   N   m

Milk!

Trace, then write.

Color each picture that begins with the N sound.

Circle each N and n.

n N H m N

M h N n n

Necklace!

Trace, then write.

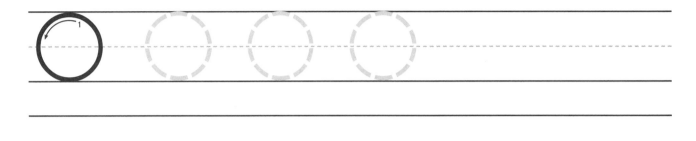

Color each picture that begins with the O sound.

Circle each O and o.

O   a   O   Q   p

o   G   o   O   o

Octagon!

46

© Scholastic Inc.

Draw lines!

Match each picture to the letter it begins with.

 Mm

 9

 Nn

Oo

Write the missing letters.

m, _____, o   m, n, _____

M, N, _____   M, _____, O

_____, n, o   _____, N, O

M= red   N= yellow   O= blue

Use the code to color the picture.

What is it?

Match the letters.

N •   • o   M •   • n

O •   • n   N •   • o

M •   • m   O •   • m

Count and graph the letters.

Say each letter!

n
m
M o n o O
N n
M m M
M o
O n o

	M	m	N	n	O	o
4						
3						
2						
1						

Great work! Bye!

Fill in the letters. Color the pictures.

M
N
O

_____ is for  .

_____ is for  .

_____ is for  .

Write the first letter for each word.

m
n
o

_____live   _____ug   _____ut

50

Trace each letter.

LETTERS
P Q R

Hi!

P
Q
R

Color in each box when you complete the activity.

1	**2**	**3**	**4**
Introduction	Pp	Qq	Rr
5	**6**	**7**	**8**
Match & Write	Color & Match	Graph	Review

Trace, then write.

P P P P

p p p p

Color each picture that begins with the P sound.

Circle each **P** and **p**.

P   q   a   B   P

p   R   P   p   b

Popcorn!

Trace, then write.

Color each picture that begins with the Q sound.

SHHH

Circle each Q and q.

O   p   Q   q   Q

q   D   q   b   Q

Quarter!

Trace, then write.

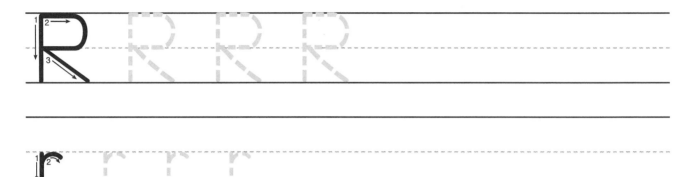

Color each picture that begins with the R sound.

Circle each R and r.

R   P   r   R   r

n   R   m   F   r

Rocket!

Draw lines!

Match each picture to the letter it begins with.

Pp

Qq

Rr

Write the missing letters.

_____, Q, R

p, _____, r

P, Q, _____

p, q, _____

P, _____, R

_____, q, r

P=  orange   Q= brown   R= green

Use the code to color the picture.

What is it?

Match the letters.

P •   • q   R •   • q

R •   • p   P •   • p

Q •   • r   Q •   • r

56

© Scholastic Inc.

Count and graph the letters.

Say each letter!

q R r

P Q r Q

Q P

R p R p

Q r q

	P	p	Q	q	R	r
4						
3						
2						
1						

Fill in the letters. Color the pictures.

P
Q
R

_____ is for .

_____ is for .

_____ is for  .

Write the first letter for each word.

p
q
r

_____ot

_____ake

_____ueen

Trace each letter.

Color in each box when you complete the activity.

1	2	3	4
Introduction	Ss	Tt	Uu
5	6	7	8
Match & Write	Color & Match	Graph	Review

Trace, then write.

S S S S

s s s s

Color each picture that begins with the S sound.

Circle each S and s.

S	P	s	g	S
p	R	s	S	s

Sandwich!

Trace, then write.

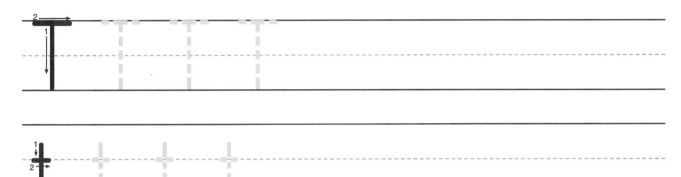

Color each picture that begins with the T sound.

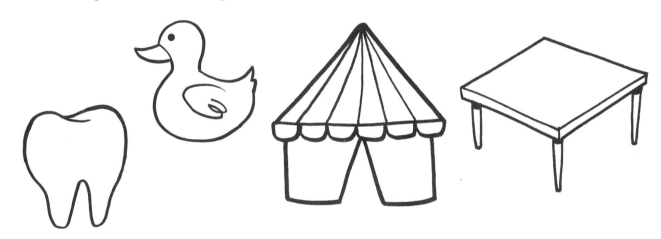

Toothbrush!

Circle each T and t.

T k T t I

L t h T t

Trace, then write.

Color each picture that begins with the U sound.

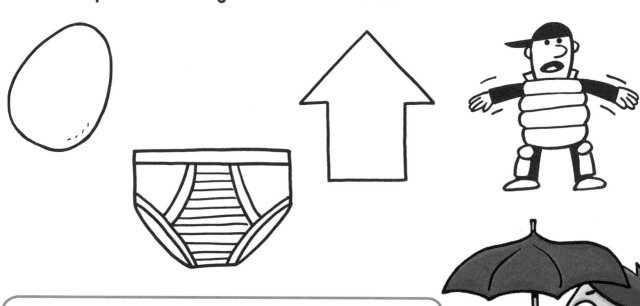

Circle each U and u.

| u | U | V | w | U |
| W | u | U | v | u |

Umbrella!

© Scholastic Inc.

Draw lines!

Match each picture to the letter it begins with.

Ss

Tt

Uu

Write the missing letters.

S, _____, U

s, _____, u

_____, T, U

S, T, _____

s, t, _____

_____, t, u

S= yellow   T= green   U= blue

Use the code to color the picture.

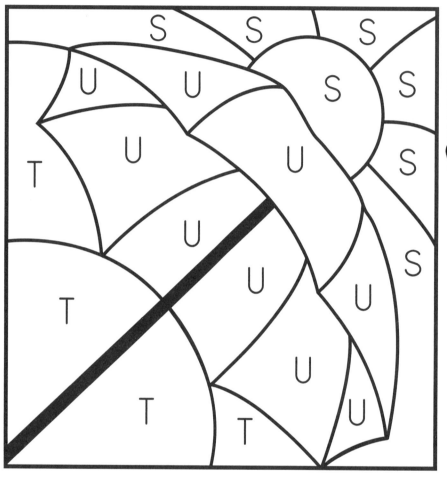

What is it?

Match the letters.

U •   • u   S •   • t

T •   • s   U •   • s

S •   • t   T •   • u

Count and graph the letters.

Say each letter!

	S	s	T	t	U	u
4						
3						
2						
1						

Great
work!
Bye!

Fill in the letters. Color the pictures.

S T U

_____ is for  .

_____ is for  .

_____ is for  .

Write the first letter for each word.

s
t
u

_____un   _____p   _____ent

Trace each letter.

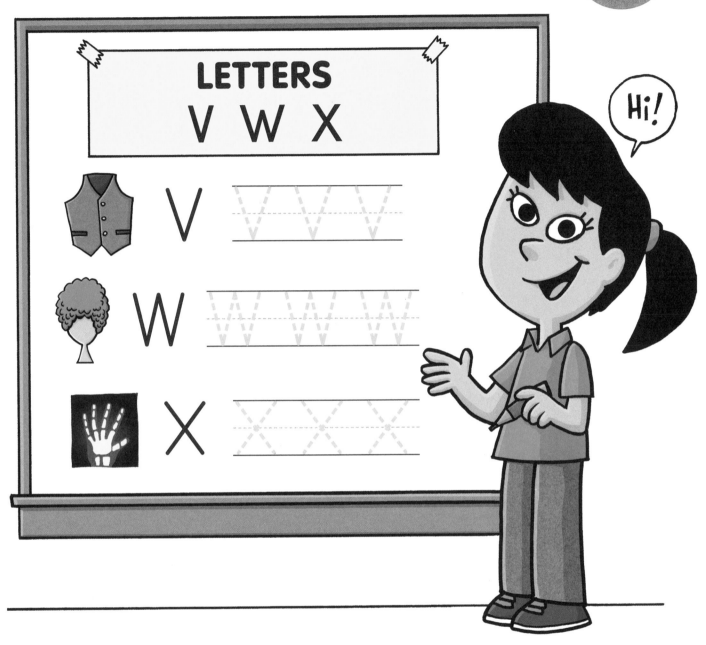

LETTERS
V W X

V

W

X

Color in each box when you complete the activity.

1 Introduction	2 Vv	3 Ww	4 Xx
5 Match & Write	6 Color & Match	7 Graph	8 Review

Trace, then write.

V V V V

V V V V

Color each picture that begins with the V sound.

Circle each V and v.

V   k   V   v   V

W   v   A   w   v

Vine!

Trace, then write.

Color each picture that begins with the W sound.

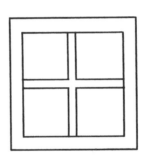

Wig!

Circle each W and w.

w	W	v	X	W
x	A	w	W	w

Trace, then write.

Color each picture that has the X sound.

Circle each X and x.

y W X x V

X x X w x

Box!

Draw lines!

Match each picture to the letter that is in that word.

 Vv

 EXIT→

 Ww

 Xx

Write the missing letters.

V, W, _____

v, w, _____

_____, w, x

_____, W, X

V, _____, X

v, _____, x

V=  brown   W= orange   X= blue

Use the code to color the picture.

What is it?

Match the letters.

X •	• v	W •	• x
W •	• x	V •	• v
V •	• w	X •	• w

Count and graph the letters.

Say each letter!

	V	v	W	w	X	x
4						
3						
2						
1						

Fill in the letters. Color the pictures.

V
W
X

_____ is for .

_____ is for  .

_____ is for  .

Write the missing letter in each word.

V
W
X

____an

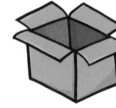

bo____

____eb

Trace each letter.

Color in each box when you complete the activity.

1 Introduction	2 Yy	3 Zz	4 Match & Write
5 Color & Match	6 Graph	7 Review	8 Alphabet Review

Trace, then write.

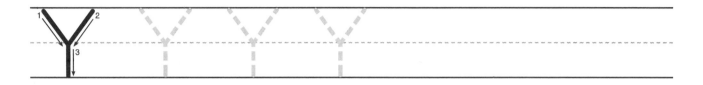

Color each picture that begins with the Y sound.

Circle each Y and y.

Y   v   W   Y   y

y   V   x   y   Y

Yo-yo!

Trace, then write.

Color each picture that begins with the Z sound.

Circle each Z and z.

z   H   T   Z   z

x   Z   z   w   Z

Zero!

77

Draw lines!

Match each picture to the letter it begins with.

Write the missing letters.

x, y, _____

x, _____, z

X, Y, _____

X, _____, Z

X, Y, _____

x, _____, z

 Y= red   Z= blue

Use the code to color the picture.

What is it?

Match the letters.

X •   • z
Z •   • y
Y •   • x

Y •   • z
X •   • x
Z •   • y

© Scholastic Inc.

79

Count and graph the letters.

X	x	Y	y	Z	z

4

3

2

1

Almost done!

Fill in the letters. Color the pictures.

Y
Z

_____ is for _____ .

_____ is for _____ .

Write the first letter for each word.

y
z

ZOO

____oo   ____arn   ____ip

Write the missing letters.

A, _____, C, D, _____, F,

_____, H, _____, _____, K,

L, M, _____, O, _____, Q,

_____, S, _____, U, _____,

W, _____, Y, _____

Great work! Bye!

Match the letters.

O •   • q

D •   • r

Q •   • o

R •   • p

P •   • d

H •   • n

A •   • a

N •   • h

V •   • w

W •   • v

Use the color code to color the picture.

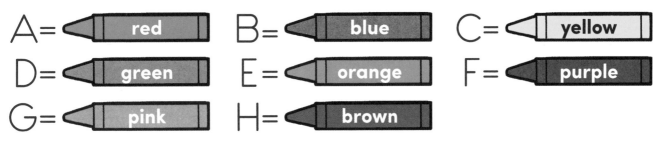

A = red

B = blue

C = yellow

D = green

E = orange

F = purple

G = pink

H = brown

Count the flowers!

Color in each box when you complete the activity.

1	2	3	4
Color by Letter	Sequencing	Connect-the-Dots	Trace the Path
5	6	7	8
Connect-the-Dots	Color the Path	Match	Match & Write

Use my alphabet chart!

A B C D E F G H I J K L M
N O P Q R S T U V W X Y Z

Fill in the missing letters. Then color the letters of your first name blue.

Connect the dots. Start at A. Hint: Look for the star.

What is it?

Feed the animals!

Trace the path from each animal to the food that begins with the same sound.

b b b e

z z e b

l e z z

e l

e l w

w w l

w

What is it?

Connect the dots. Start at a. Hint: Look for the star.

Color the path from a to z.

Match each shoe to its mate.

Draw lines!

SHOE SALE!

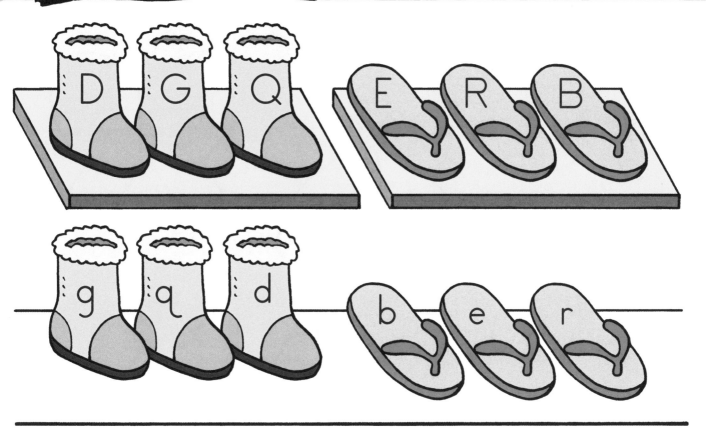

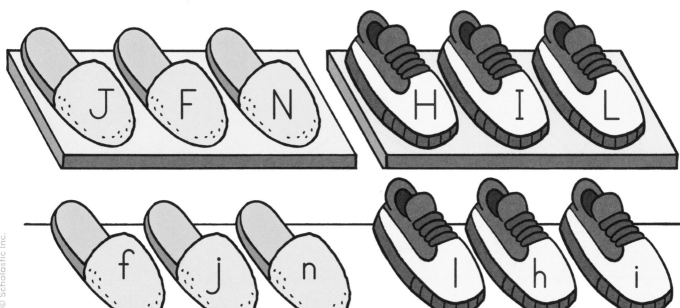

Write the matching letter on each bug.
Use the letters in the box. Then color the bug.

m   p   s   t   v   w   x   y   z

W __

T __

M __

Y __

X __

S __

P __

Great
work!
Bye!

V __

Z __

EARLY LEARNING

NUMBERS

Family Activities

Here are some skill-building activities that you and your child might enjoy.

Project Count

Choose items in your home, such as picture frames or books. Walk around your home with your child and count how many you can find.

How Many Steps?

Challenge your child to guess how many steps it takes to go from the front door to your kitchen or from the bedroom to the bathroom. Then have your child walk heel-to-toe and count the number of steps. Ask your child: *Do you think it would take more or fewer steps if I (or another grown-up) measured the distance the same way?*

How Many in Our Family?

Make counting more meaningful to your child by asking: *How many feet are there in our family? How many eyes? How many fingers in our family?*

Cereal Math

Use candy or cereal to help reinforce the concept of addition and subtraction. For example, ask: *If I have two pieces of cereal and you have one, how many do we both have?* Help your child count the total number of pieces.

NUMBERS
1 2 3

Hi!

Trace each number.

1

2

3

Color each box when you complete that page.

1 Introduction	2 Count & Color	3 Count & Draw	4 Match & Write
5 Sequence & Compare	6 Compare & Add	7 Trace & Match	8 Review

Say each number. Color that many balls.

Count the balls!

Use the code to color the cars.

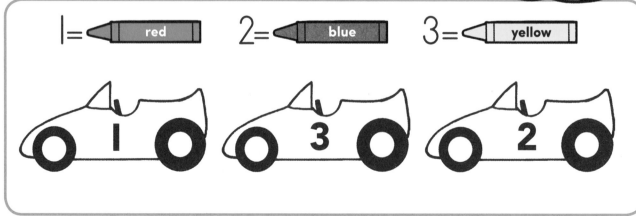

1 = red   2 = blue   3 = yellow

Count the fish. Circle the number.

1 2 3

1 2 3

Draw 2 fish in the fish tank.

Count your fish!

Count the flowers!

Match each number to its set.

1 •   •

2 •   •

3 •   •

How many? Write the number.

Write the missing numbers.

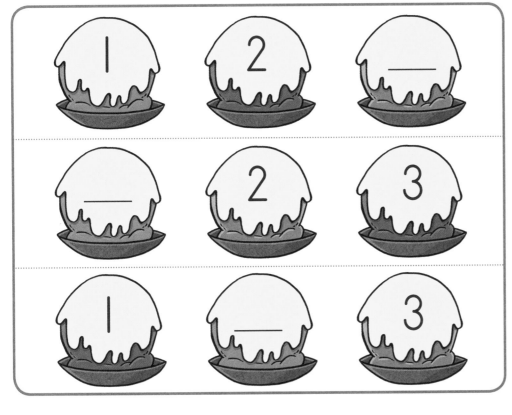

Say the numbers!

Color each cone that has more scoops.

Count the bugs!

Circle each set that has fewer bugs.

  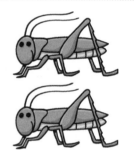

Write one more. Use the number line to help you. Then add.

START HERE.

0   1   2   3

Number	1 more
1	
0	
2	

Add.

1 + 1 = _____

0 + 1 = _____

2 + 1 = _____

Trace each number word.

1

2 two two

3 three three

Read each word!

Match each number to its name.

 2 •

       3 •

 | •

      • one

      • two

      • three

Trace each number and word. Draw a set of balls in the box.

1   1 one

2   2 two

3   3 three

How many? Write the number. Circle the set that has more.

Great work!
Bye!

NUMBERS
4 5 6

Trace each number.

4

5

6

Hi!

Color each box when you complete that page.

1 Introduction	2 Count & Color	3 Count & Draw	4 Match & Write
5 Sequence & Compare	6 Compare & Add	7 Trace & Match	8 Review

Say each number. Color that many toys.

Count the toys!

Use the code to color the cars.

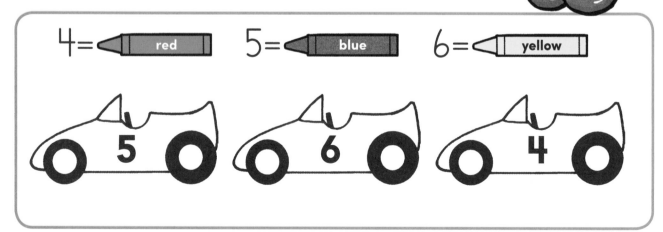

$4 =$ red $5 =$ blue $6 =$ yellow

Count the fish. Circle the number.

4 5 6

4 5 6

Draw 4 fish in the fish tank.

Count your fish!

Count the fruits!

Match each number to its set.

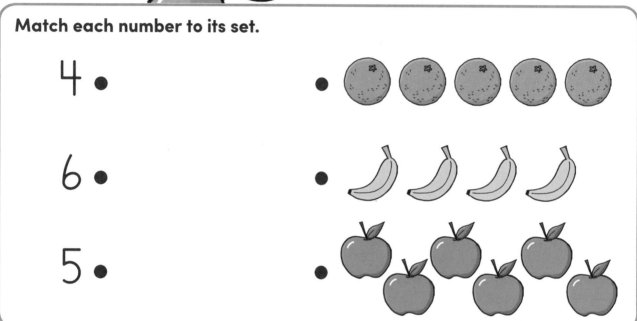

4 •

6 •

5 •

How many? Write the number.

Write the missing numbers.

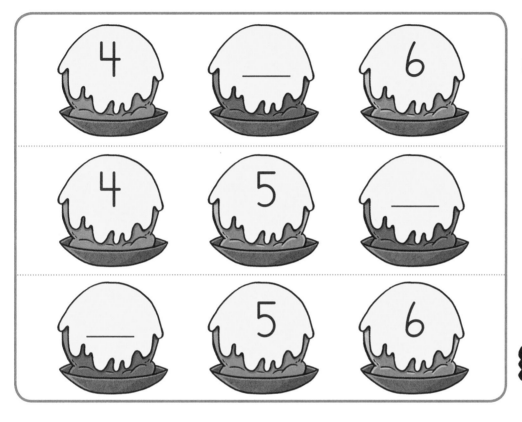

Say the numbers!

Color each sundae that has more chocolate chips.

Count the bugs!

Circle each set that has fewer bugs.

  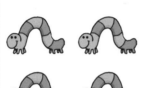 

Write one more. Use the number line to help you. Then add.

START HERE.

0   1   2   3   4   5   6

Number	1 more		Add.
4		➡	4 + 1 = _____
3		➡	3 + 1 = _____
5		➡	5 + 1 = _____

Trace each number word.

4 four four

5 five five

6 six six

Read each word!

Match each number to its name.

 5 •

• five

 6 •

• four

 4 •

• six

Trace each number and word. Draw a set of balls in the box.

4   4 four

5   5 five

6   6 six

How many? Write the number. Circle the set that has more.

Great work! Bye!

NUMBERS
7 8 9

Trace each number.

7

8

9

Hi!

Color each box when you complete that page.

1 Introduction	2 Count & Color	3 Count & Draw	4 Match & Write
5 Sequence & Compare	6 Compare & Add	7 Trace & Match	8 Review

Say each number. Color that many balls.

Count the
balls!

Use the code to color the cars.

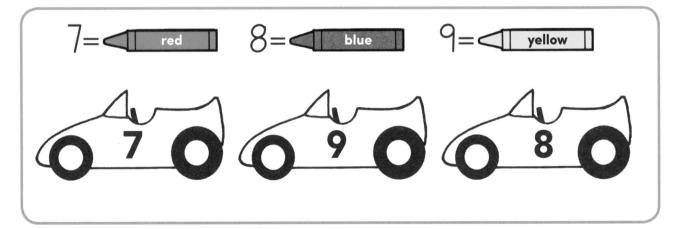

$7 =$ red $\quad 8 =$ blue $\quad 9 =$ yellow

7   9   8

Count the fish. Circle the number.

7 8 9

7 8 9

Draw 8 fish in the fish tank.

Count your fish!

Count the kites!

Match each number to its set.

8 •

7 •

9 •

How many? Write the number.

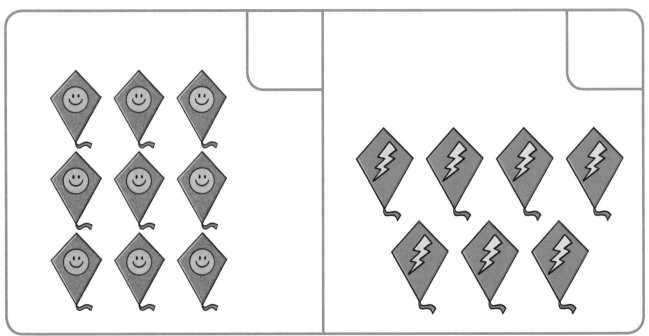

Write the missing numbers.

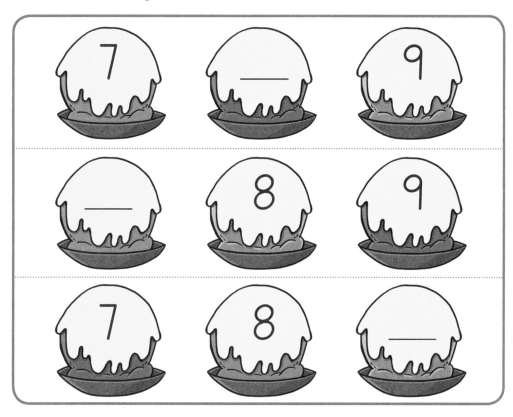

Say the numbers!

YUM ICE CREAM

Color each cone that has more scoops.

Count the school tools!

Circle each set that has fewer tools.

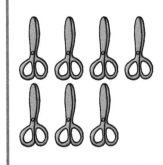
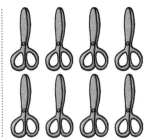
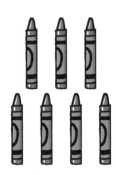
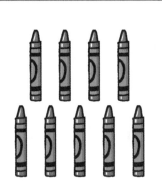

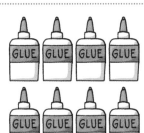
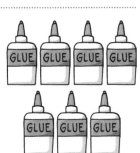

Write one more. Use the number line to help you. Then add.

START HERE.

0 1 2 3 4 5 6 7 8 9

Number	1 more		Add.
8		➔	8 + 1 = _____
7		➔	7 + 1 = _____
6		➔	6 + 1 = _____

Count the fish. Circle the number.

Draw 11 fish in the fish tank.

Count your fish!

Count the pets!

Match each number to its set.

2 •

10 •

11 •

•

How many? Write the number.

Write the missing numbers.

Say the numbers!

YUM
ICE
CREAM

Color each cone that has more scoops.

Count the hats!

Circle the set that has fewer hats.

Write one more. Use the number line to help you. Then add.

START HERE.

0 1 2 3 4 5 6 7 8 9 10 11 12

Number	1 more		Add.
10		➡	10 + 1 = _____
9		➡	9 + 1 = _____
11		➡	11 + 1 = _____

122

© Scholastic Inc.

Trace each number word.

10

11

12

Read each word!

Match each number to its name.

12 •   • ten

10 •   • twelve

11 •   • eleven

Trace each number and word. Draw a set of balls in the box.

10   10 ten

11   11 eleven

12   12 twelve

How many? Write the number. Circle the set that has more.

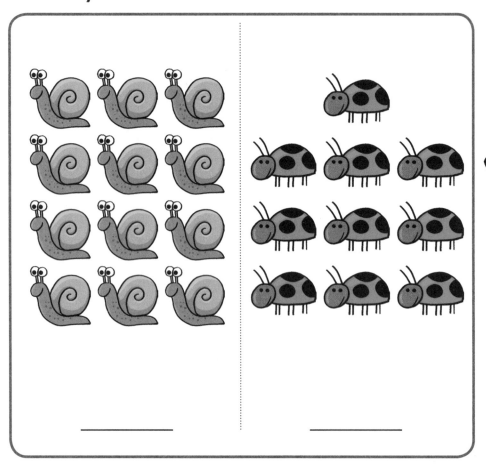

Great work! Bye!

124

© Scholastic Inc.

NUMBERS
13 14 15

Hi!

Trace each number.

13

14

15

Color each box when you complete that page.

1	2	3	4
Introduction	**Count & Color**	**Count & Draw**	**Match & Write**
5	6	7	8
Sequence & Compare	**Compare & Add**	**Trace & Match**	**Review**

Say each number. Color that many balls.

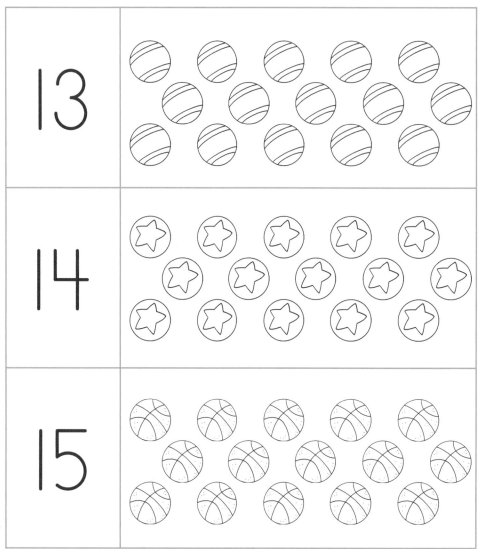

Count the balls!

Use the code to color the cars.

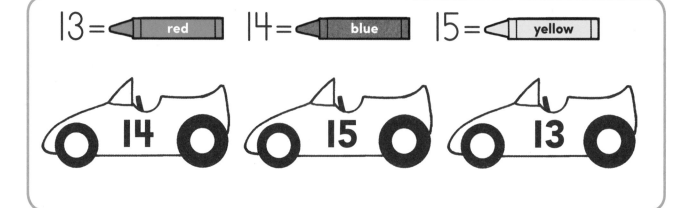

Count the fish. Circle the number.

Draw 14 fish in the fish tank.

Count your fish!

Count the toys!

Match each number to its set.

15 •

13 •

14 •

•

•

•

How many? Write the number.

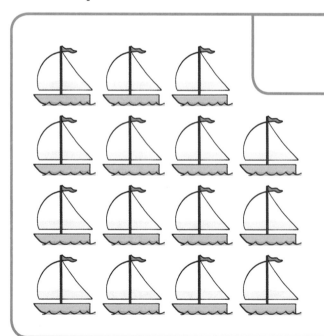

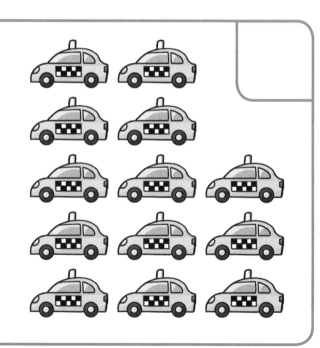

Write the missing numbers.

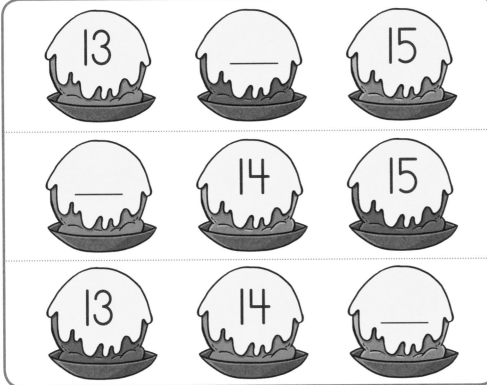

Say the numbers!

YUM ICE CREAM

Color the sundae that has more chocolate chips.

Count the gifts!

Circle the set that has fewer gifts.

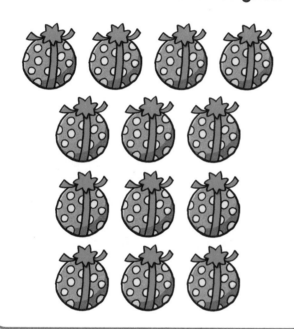

Write one more. Use the number line to help you. Then add.

START HERE.

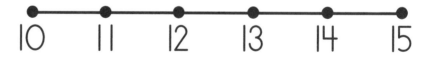

| 10 | 11 | 12 | 13 | 14 | 15 |

Number	1 more	Add.
14		14 + 1 = _____
12		12 + 1 = _____
13		13 + 1 = _____

Trace each number word.

13 ___thirteen___

14 ___fourteen___

15 ___fifteen___

Read each word!

Match each number to its name.

13 •

• thirteen

14 •

• fifteen

15 •

• fourteen

Trace each number and word. Draw a set of balls in the box.

13   13 thirteen

14   14 fourteen

15   15 fifteen

How many? Write the number. Circle the set that has more.

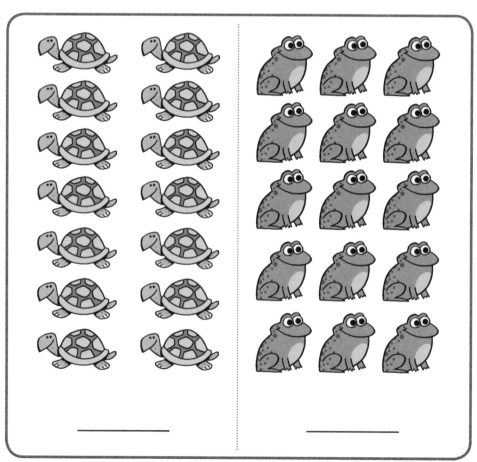

Great work! Bye!

NUMBERS

16 17 18

Hi!

Trace each number.

16

17

18

Color each box when you complete that page.

1	2	3	4
Introduction	Count & Color	Count & Draw	Match & Write
5	6	7	8
Sequence & Compare	Compare & Add	Trace & Match	Review

Say each number. Color that many toys.

18	
16	
17	

Use the code to color the cars.

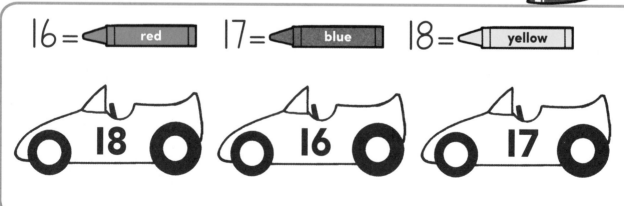

16 = red 17 = blue 18 = yellow

18   16   17

Count the fish. Circle the number.

16   17   18

16   17   18

Draw 17 fish in the fish tank.

Count your fish!

Count the foods!

Match each number to its set.

16 •

17 •

18 •

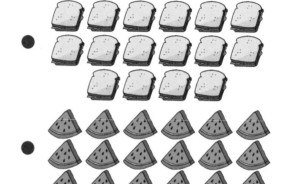

How many? Write the number.

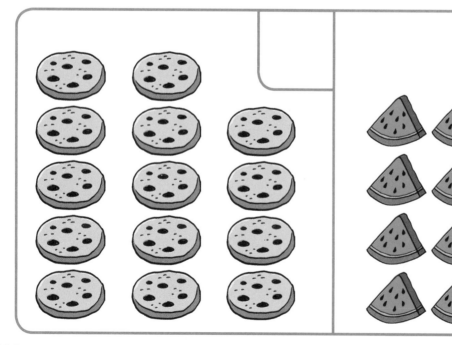

Write the missing numbers.

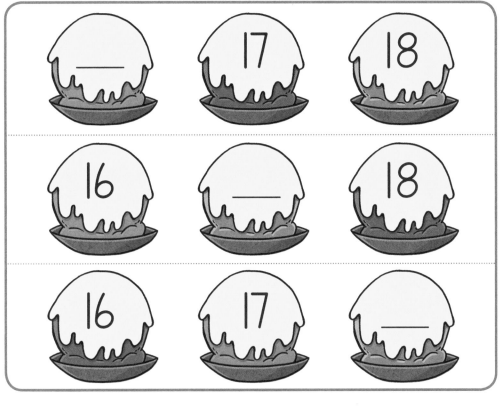

Say the numbers!

Color the sundae that has more chocolate chips.

Count the buttons!

Circle the set that has fewer buttons.

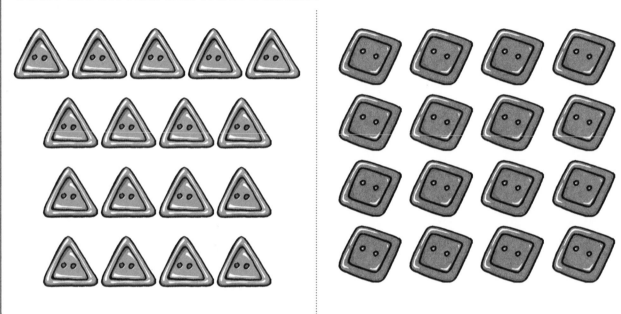

Write one more. Use the number line to help you. Then add.

START HERE.

10   11   12   13   14   15   16   17   18

Number	1 more		Add.
16		➡	16 + 1 = _____
15		➡	15 + 1 = _____
17		➡	17 + 1 = _____

138

Trace each number word.

16 ——sixteen——

17 ——seventeen——

18 ——eighteen——

Read each word!

Match each number to its name.

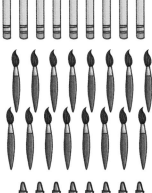

18 •

16 •

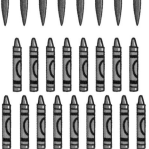

17 •

• sixteen

• eighteen

• seventeen

Trace each number and word. Draw a set of balls in the box.

16 16 sixteen

17 17 seventeen

18 18 eighteen

How many? Write the number. Circle the set that has more.

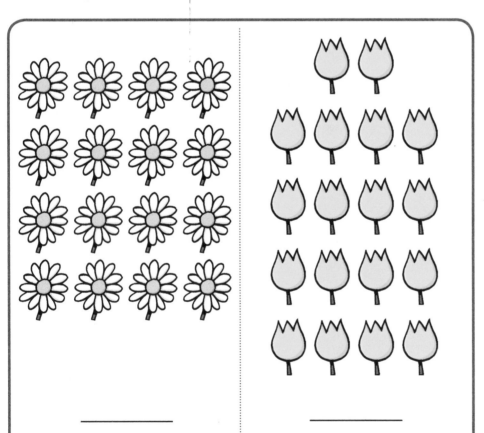

_____   _____

Great work! Bye!

NUMBERS
19 20

Hi!

Trace each number.

19

20

Color each box when you complete that page.

| 1 Introduction | 2 Count & Color | 3 Count & Draw | 4 Match & Write |
| 5 Sequence & Compare | 6 Compare & Add | 7 Trace & Match | 8 Review |

Say each number. Color that many animals.

Count the animals!

Use the code to color the cars.

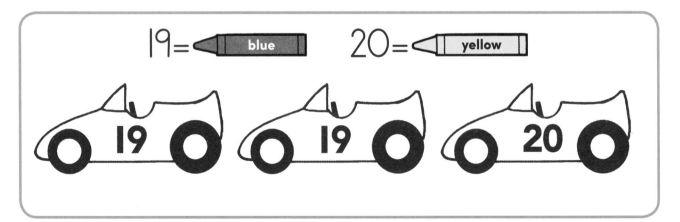

19 = blue 20 = yellow

Count the fish. Circle the number.

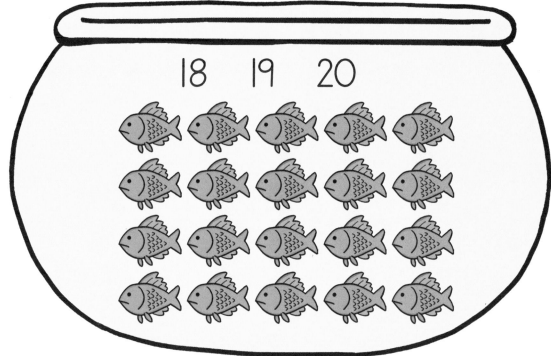

18   19   20

Draw 19 fish in the fish tank.

Count your fish!

Count the flowers!

Match each number to its set.

19 •

20 •

•

How many? Write the number.

Write the missing numbers.

Say the numbers!

YUM ICE CREAM

Color the sundae that has more chocolate chips.

Count the bugs!

Circle the set that has fewer bugs.

Write one more. Use the number line to help you. Then add.

START HERE.

10 11 12 13 14 15 16 17 18 19 20

Number	1 more	Add.
18		18 + 1 = _____
17		17 + 1 = _____
19		19 + 1 = _____

146

Trace each number word.

19

nineteen nineteen

20

twenty twenty

Read each word!

Match each number to its name.

19 •   • twenty

20 •   • nineteen

Trace each number and word. Draw a set of balls in the box.

19 19 nineteen

20 20 twenty

How many? Write the number. Circle the set that has fewer.

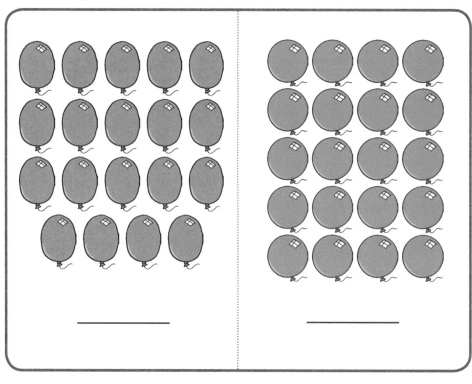

_____   _____

Great work!
Bye!

NUMBERS
1 to 100

Hi!

Trace each number and the number word.

100   100

one hundred

Color each box when you complete that page.

1	2	3	4
Introduction	1 to 20	21 to 40	41 to 60
5	6	7	8
61 to 80	81 to 100	1 to 100	Review

Write the missing numbers.

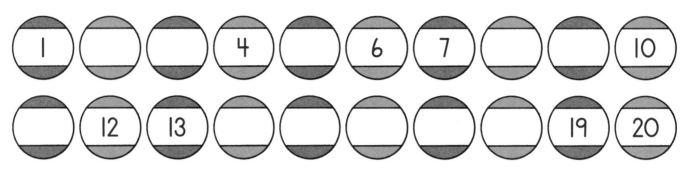

| 1 | | | 4 | | 6 | 7 | | | 10 |

| | 12 | 13 | | | | | | 19 | 20 |

Count the cars!

Say each number. Color that many cars.

17	
11	
20	
9	

Trace each number and number word.

30 30 thirty thirty

40 40 forty forty

Write the missing numbers.

21 · 23 · · · 26 27 · 29 ·

· 32 · 34 · · 37 · · 40

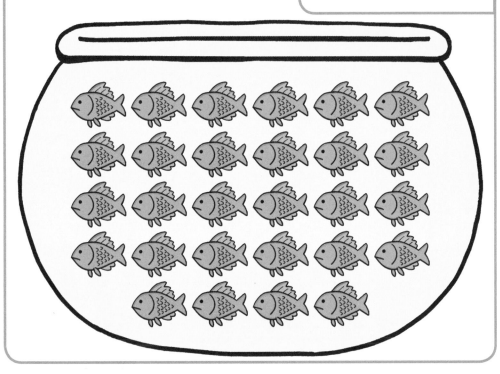

How many? Circle the number.

28   35   39

Say each number!

Trace each number and number word.

50   50   fifty   fifty

60   60   sixty   sixty

Write the missing numbers.

 42 43   46 48 49

51   54   57   60

How many? Write the number.

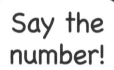

Say the number!

Trace each number and number word.

70 70 seventy

80 80 eighty

Write the missing numbers.

| | 62 | | | 65 | | 67 | | | 70 |

| 71 | | | 74 | | 76 | | | 79 | |

How many chocolate chips? Write the number.

Say the number!

Trace each number and number word.

90 90 ninety

100 100 one hundred

Write the missing numbers.

82 · 85 · · 89 90

· 93 · · 96 · 98 · ·

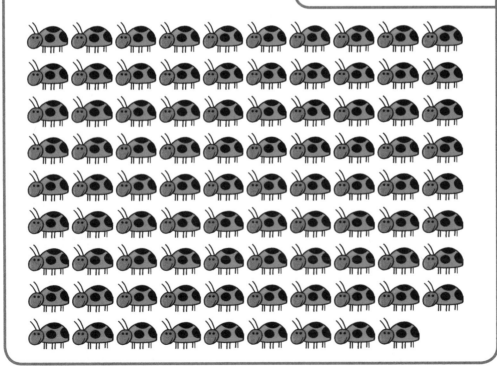

How many? Circle the number. 79 89 98

Say each number!

Say each number!

Write the missing numbers.

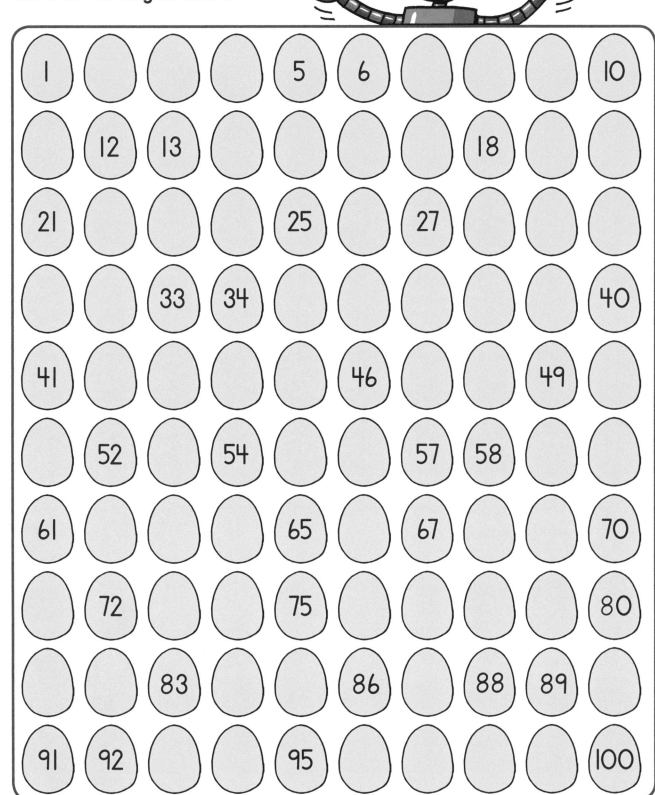

				5	6				10
12	13					18		
21			25		27			
	33	34						40
41				46			49	
52		54			57	58		
61			65		67			70
72			75					80
	83			86		88	89	
91	92		95					100

Write the missing numbers.

39   _____   _____   42   _____

_____   97   _____   99   _____

71   _____   73   _____   75

Which number is more? Color that butterfly.

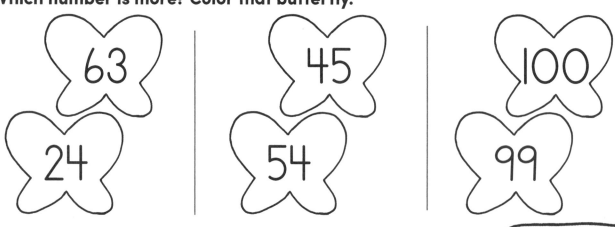

63   45   100

24   54   99

How many? Write the number.

Great work! Bye!

NUMBERS

10s to 100

Trace each number.

Hi!

Color each box when you complete that page.

1	2	3	4
Introduction	20, 30, 40	50, 60, 70	80, 90, 100

5	6	7	8
Sequence & Compare	Compare & Add	Count & Color	Review

Match each number to its set.

40 •

•

20 •

•

30 •

•

Count the toys!

How many? Write the number.

Match each number to its set.

70 •

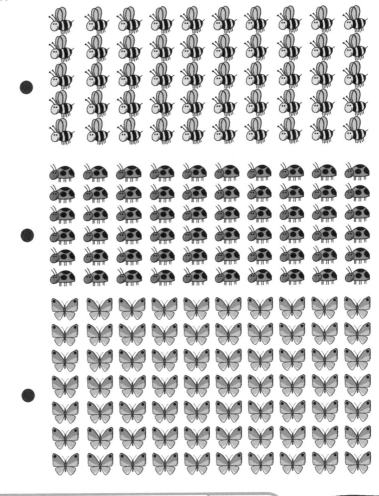

60 •

50 •

How many? Write the number.

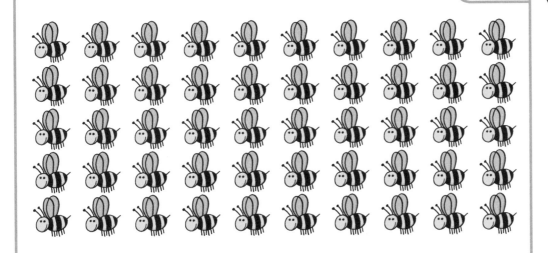

Say the number!

Match each number to its set.

100 •

80 •

90 •

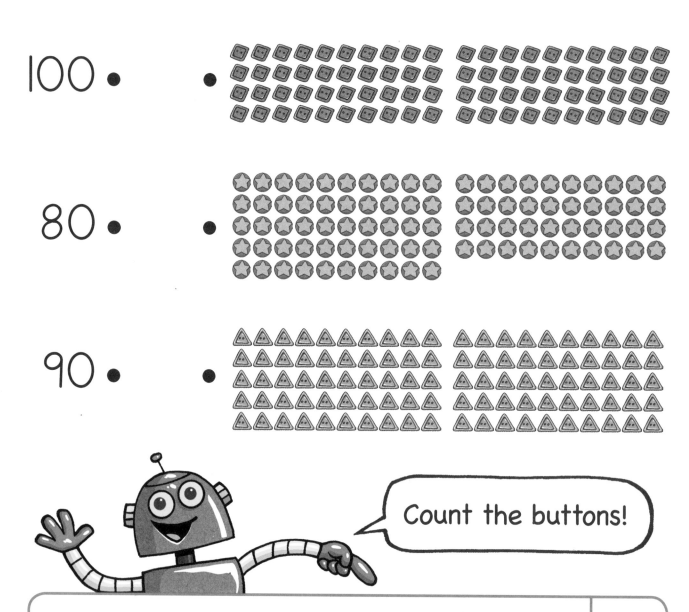

Count the buttons!

How many? Write the number.

Count by tens. Write the missing numbers.

40 ___ 60

80 90 ___

___ 40 50

Say the numbers!

YUM ICE CREAM

How many chocolate chips? Write the number.
Color the sundae that has more chocolate chips.

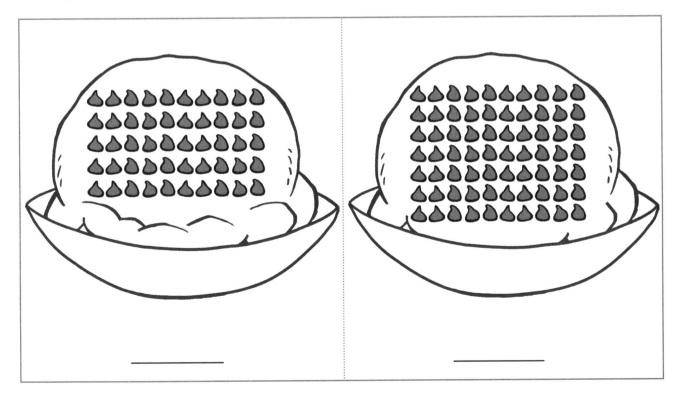

___

___

161

Count the bugs!

Circle the set that has fewer bugs.

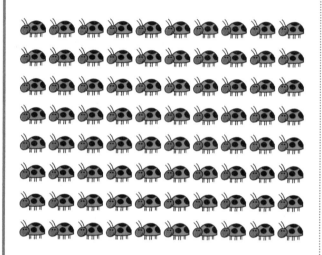

Write ten more. Use the number line to help you. Then add.

START
HERE.

10 20 30 40 50 60 70 80 90 100

Number	10 more		Add.
50		→	50 + 10 = _____
80		→	80 + 10 = _____
20		→	20 + 10 = _____

Say each number. Color that many balls.

| 70 | ○○○○○○○○○○ ○○○○○○○○○○
 ○○○○○○○○○○ ○○○○○○○○○○
 ○○○○○○○○○○ ○○○○○○○○○○
 ○○○○○○○○○○ ○○○○○○○○○○
 ○○○○○○○○○○ ○○○○○○○○○○ |
| 100 | ... |

Use the code to color the cars.

Say each number!

thirty= red   forty= blue   fifty= yellow
sixty= green   eighty= orange   ninety= purple

Trace each number. Then write the missing numbers.

10   20   ____   ____   50

60   ____   ____   90   ____

How many? Write the number. Circle the set that has more.

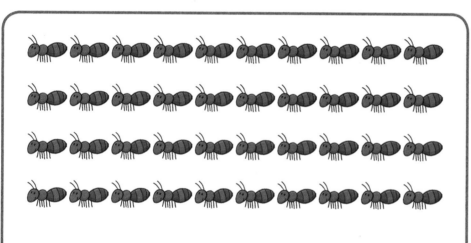

_____

_____

Great work! Bye!

Use the code to color the picture.

red
blue
yellow
green
orange
purple
black
brown
pink

Hi!

Color each box when you complete that page.

1	**2**	**3**	**4**
Count & Color	Number Words	Connect-the-Dots	Sequence & Color
5	**6**	**7**	**8**
Complete the Path	Connect-the-Dots	Color by Number	Count & Write

Read the number word. Write that number on the ice cream.

five

two

eight

four

one

six

Read each word!

ten

three

nine

seven

Connect the dots. Start at 1.
Hint: Look for the star.

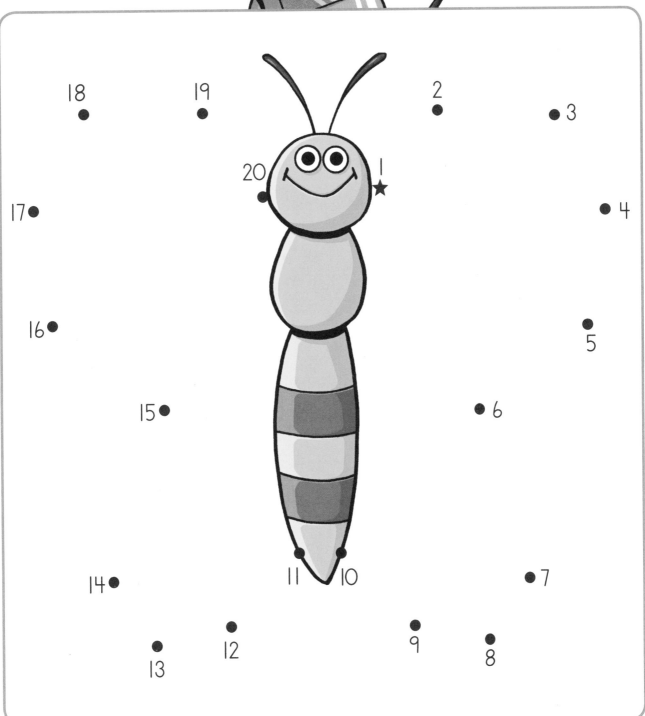

| 1 | 2 | 3 | 4 | 5 | 6 | 7 | 8 | 9 | 10 |
| 11 | 12 | 13 | 14 | 15 | 16 | 17 | 18 | 19 | 20 |

Write the missing numbers.
Then use the code to color the ants.

If the ant has a	7	10	16	19
Color the ant	red	yellow	orange	brown

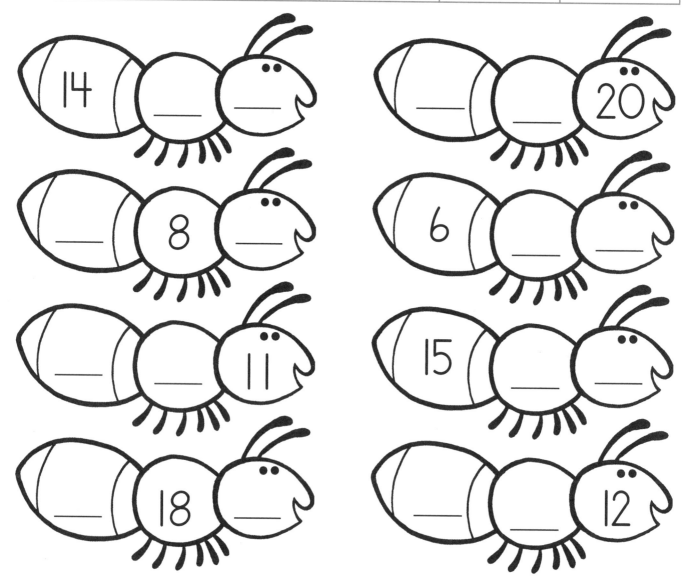

Fill in the missing numbers from 21 to 40.

Help me get to school!

Connect each set of dots. Start at 41 and 51.
Hint: Look for the stars.

45

46

43   44

47

• 48

42

49

★
41   50

Say the numbers
in order!

51 ★

60   59
• 58

52

57

53

54

55

56

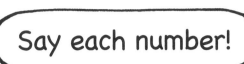

Say each number!

Use the code to color the picture.

If the number is from	Color the space
61 to 70	red
71 to 80	blue
81 to 90	yellow
91 to 100	orange

73

93

82

95

91

84

96

86

77

78

83

64

88

69

85

71

61

81

68

75

100

100

Great work! Bye!

Count the bees. Write the number on each hive.

How many?

How many is **1 more?**

How many?

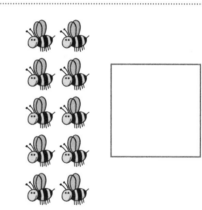

How many is **10 more?**

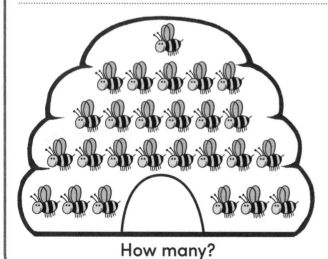

How many?

How many is **1 more?**

EARLY LEARNING
BASIC SKILLS

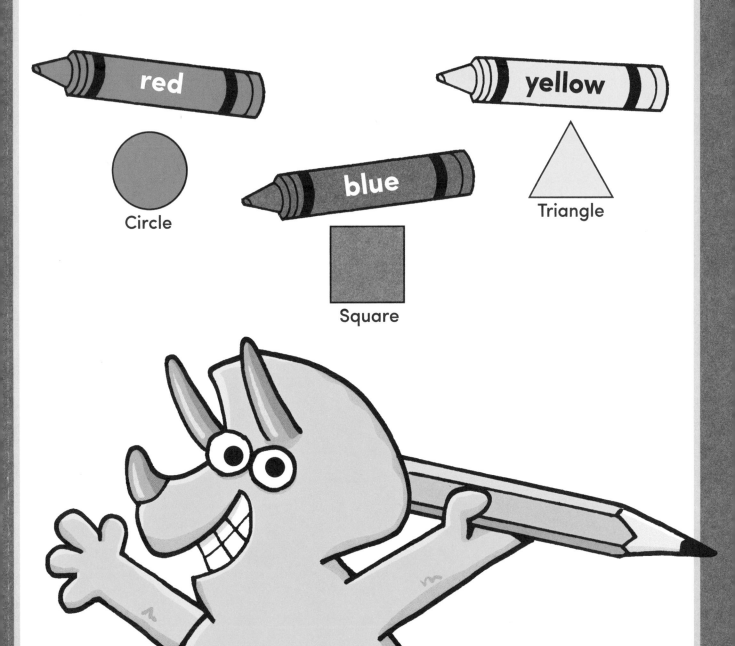

red

yellow

blue

Circle

Triangle

Square

Family Activities

Here are some skill-building activities that you and your child might enjoy.

Name the Color

When eating colorful foods such as fruits and vegetables, have your child name the colors they see. Continue by asking your child to name the color of his or her favorite fruits and vegetables.

Build Shapes

Using gumdrops or marshmallows and toothpicks, or ice cream sticks and glue, encourage your child to build different shapes, such as triangles, squares, or rectangles.

Patterns Everywhere!

Patterns are all around us. Being able to recognize these patterns is an essential skill. Help your child find patterns in an article of clothing that a family member is wearing. Alternatively, provide your child with a sheet of paper and crayons and have him or her create a pattern.

Button Sort

Gather a collection of buttons and invite your child to sort the buttons by different attributes. For example, your child can sort the buttons by color, by the number of holes, and so on.

Color each crayon.

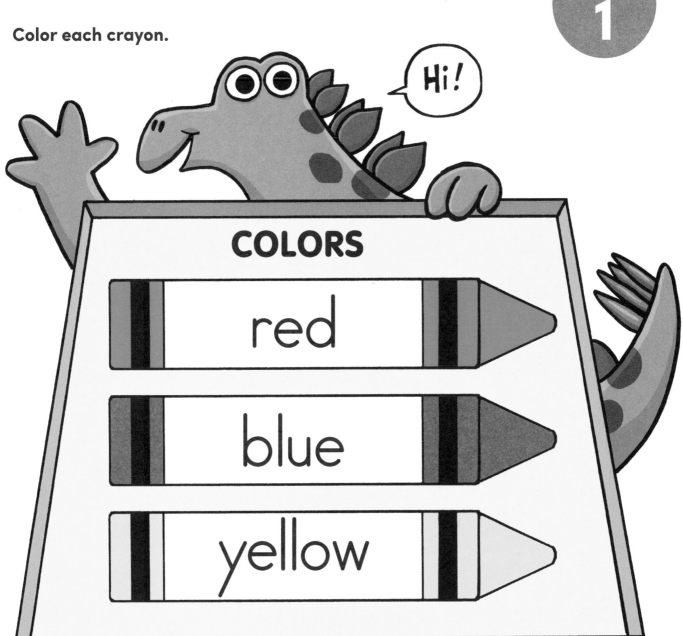

Color in each box when you complete that page.

1 Introduction	2 Trace & Color: Red	3 Trace & Color: Blue	4 Trace & Color: Yellow
5 Match & Color	6 Color by Code	7 Graph	8 Review

Color my pinwheel red!

Trace with red.

red red red red

Color each picture red.

176

Trace with blue.

blue blue blue blue

Color each picture blue.

Color my flower yellow!

Trace with yellow.

Color each picture yellow.

Color the pictures!

Match each picture to its color in real life.

red

blue

yellow

© Scholastic Inc.

Use the code to color the picture.

What is it?

● blue ■ yellow ▲ red

Color, count, and graph the foods.

= red = blue = yellow

Use the color code!

	red	blue	yellow
4			
3			
2			
1			

Read each color name. Use that color to trace the word.

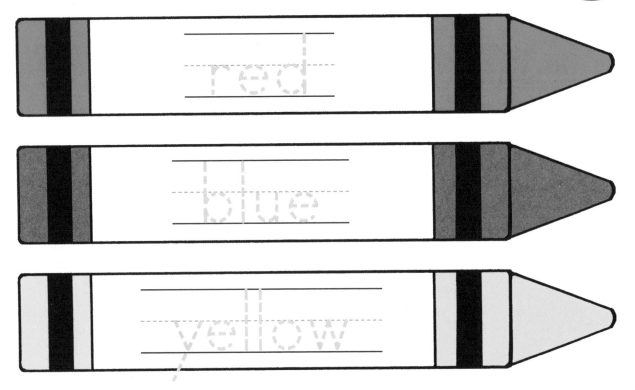

red

blue

yellow

Color each item the color it is in real life. Use red, blue, and yellow.

STOP

Great work! Bye!

Color each crayon.

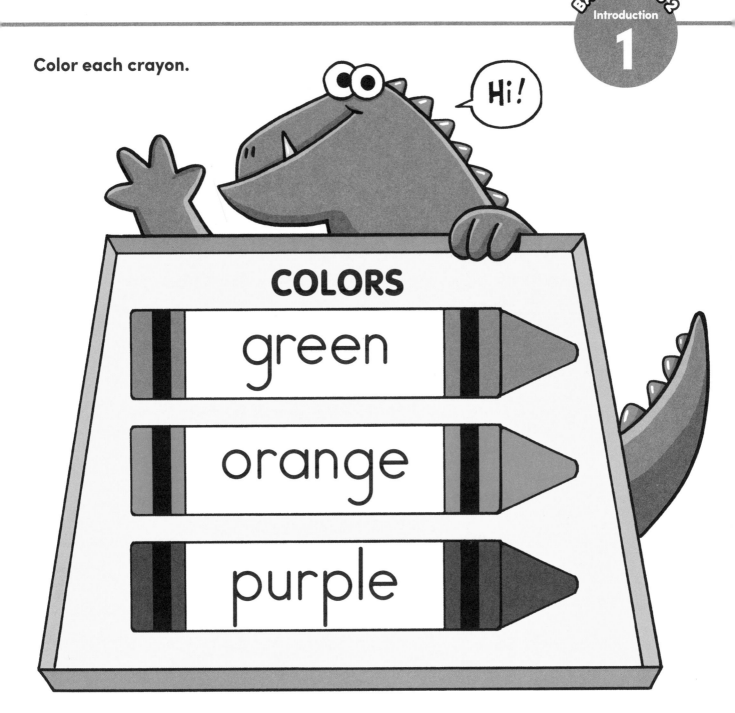

Color in each box when you complete that page.

1 Introduction	2 Trace & Color: Green	3 Trace & Color: Orange	4 Trace & Color: Purple
5 Match & Color	6 Color by Code	7 Graph	8 Review

Color my clover green!

Trace with green.

green green green

Color each picture green.

Color my pumpkin orange!

Trace with orange.

orange   orange

Color each picture orange.

Color my lollipop purple!

Trace with purple.

purple   purple

Color each picture purple.

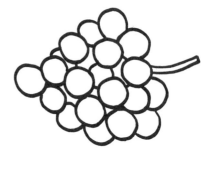

GRAPE

Color the pictures!

Match each picture to its color in real life.

orange

green

purple

Use the code to color the picture.

What is it?

● ◄ purple   ■ ◄ green   ▲ ◄ orange

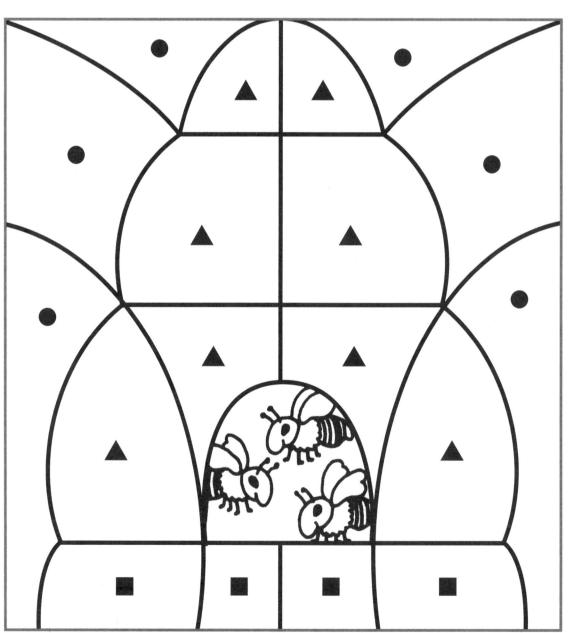

Color, count, and graph the foods.

= green   = orange   = purple

Use the color code!

	green	orange	purple
4			
3			
2			
1			

Read each color name. Use that color to trace the word.

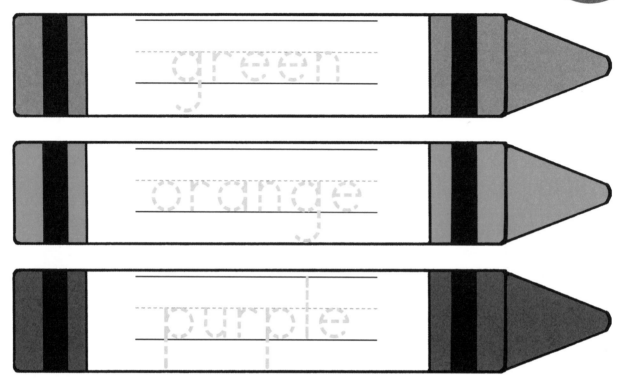

Color each item the color it is in real life. Use green, orange, and purple.

Great work! Bye!

Color each crayon.

COLORS

white

brown

black

Color in each box when you complete that page.

1 Introduction	**2** Trace & Color: White	**3** Trace & Color: Brown	**4** Trace & Color: Black
5 Match & Color	**6** Color by Code	**7** Graph	**8** Review

Color my popcorn white!

Trace with white.

white   white   white

Color each picture white.

Color my ice cream brown!

Trace with brown.

brown   brown

Color each picture brown.

Color my blackberries black!

Trace with black.

black   black   black

Color each picture black.

Color the pictures!

Match each picture to its color in real life.

black

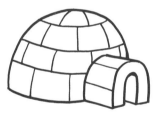

brown

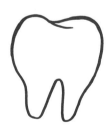

white

19

Use the code to color the picture.

Count the white balloons!

● black   ■ white   ▲ brown

Color, count, and graph the foods.

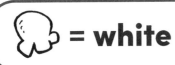 = **white**   = **brown**   = **black**

Use the color code!

	white	brown	black
4			
3			
2			
1			

Read each color name. Use that color to trace the word.

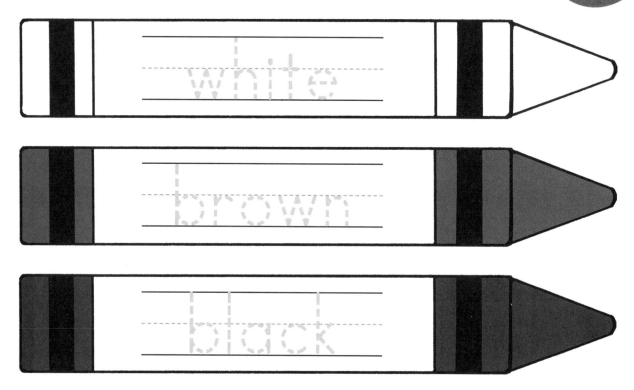

Color each item the color it is in real life. Use white, brown, and black.

Great work! Bye!

Trace each shape.

Color in each box when you complete that page.

1 Introduction	2 Trace: Circle	3 Trace: Square	4 Trace: Triangle
5 Match & Color	6 Trace & Match	7 Graph	8 Review

Trace each circle.

This is a circle!

Circle

Trace each square.

This is a
square!

Square

Trace each triangle.

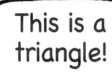
This is a triangle!

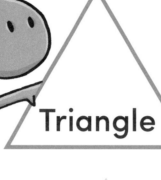

Triangle

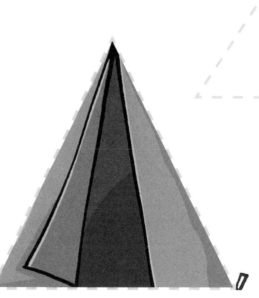

202

 Draw lines!

Match each object to its shape.

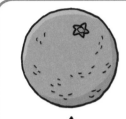

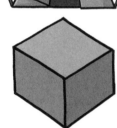

Use the code to color the shapes.

 = red   = blue   ◻ = yellow

Trace each shape word.

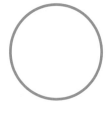 circle c̶i̶r̶c̶l̶e̶

 square s̶q̶u̶a̶r̶e̶

 triangle t̶r̶i̶a̶n̶g̶l̶e̶

Draw lines!

Match each shape to its name.

    • triangle •   

    • square •   

    • circle •   

Count and graph the objects by shape.

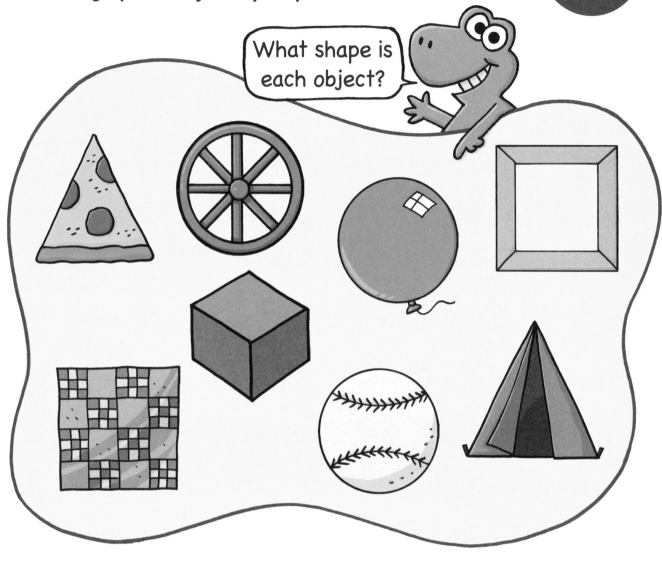

What shape is each object?

	circle	square	triangle
4			
3			
2			
1			

Trace and match.

●

●

●

Draw each shape.

circle	square	triangle

Great work!
Bye!

Trace each shape.

SHAPES

Oval

Rectangle

Hexagon

Hi!

Color in each box when you complete that page.

1 Introduction	2 Trace: Oval	3 Trace: Rectangle	4 Trace: Hexagon
5 Match & Color	6 Trace & Match	7 Graph	8 Review

Trace each oval.

This is an oval!

Oval

Trace each rectangle.

This is a rectangle!

Rectangle

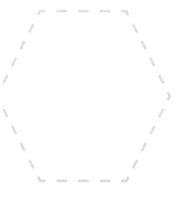

Trace each hexagon.

This is a hexagon!

Hexagon

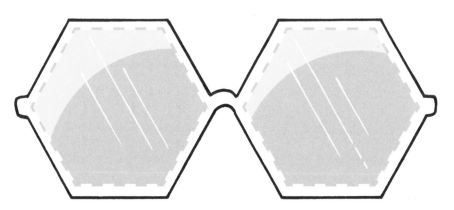

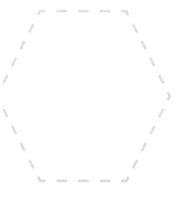

210

Draw lines!

Match each object to its shape.

Use the code to color the shapes.

= red   = blue   = yellow

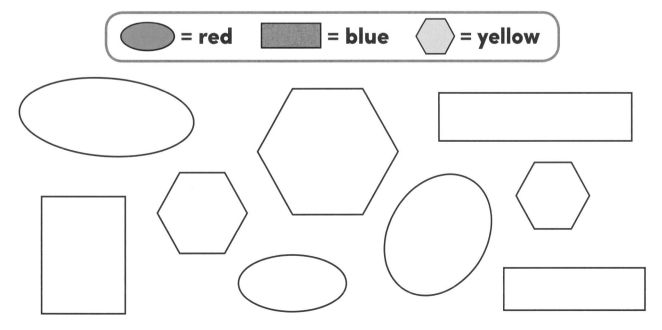

Trace each shape word.

 oval

 rectangle

hexagon

 Draw lines!

Match each shape to its name.

 • oval •

 • rectangle •

 • hexagon •

Count and graph the objects by shape.

What shape is each object?

	oval	**rectangle**	**hexagon**
4			
3			
2			
1			

Trace and match.

oval  ●

rectangle ●

hexagon ●

Draw each shape.

oval	rectangle	hexagon

Great work! Bye!

© Scholastic Inc.

Trace to complete each pattern.

PATTERNS

AB

AAB

AABB

ABC

Color in each box when you complete that page.

1	2	3	4
Introduction	AB Patterns	AAB Patterns	AABB Patterns
5	6	7	8
ABC Patterns	Complete the Patterns	Growing Patterns	Review

215

These are AB patterns!

What comes next? Color that picture.

Draw shapes to complete each pattern.

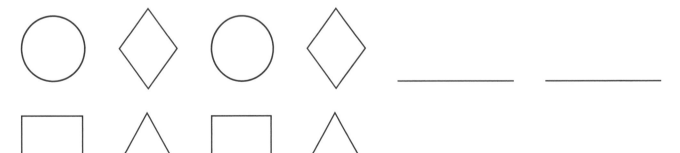

These are
AAB patterns!

What comes next? Color that picture.

Draw shapes to complete each pattern.

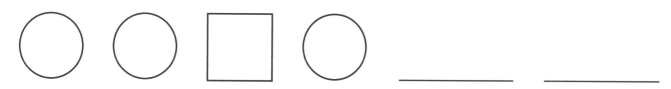

These are AABB patterns!

What comes next? Color that picture.

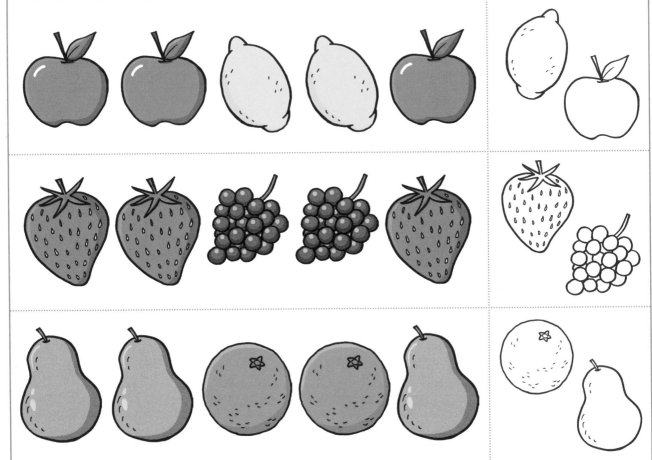

Draw shapes to complete each pattern.

These are ABC patterns!

What comes next? Color that picture.

Draw shapes to complete each pattern.

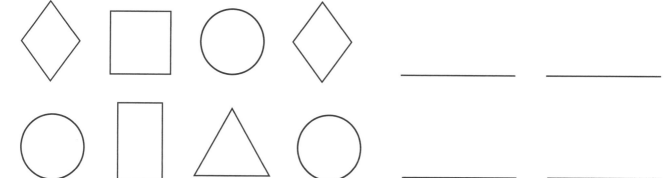

219

What comes next?

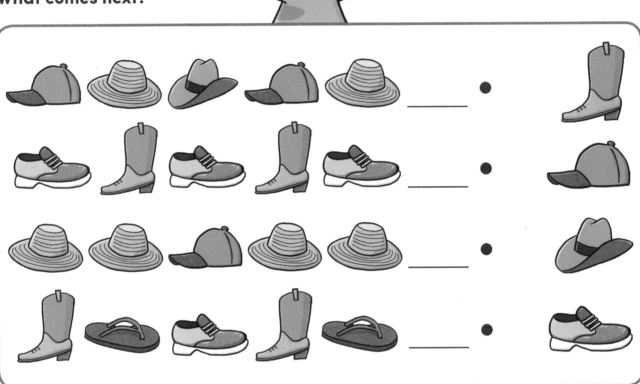

Draw pictures to complete each pattern.

_____ _____

_____ _____ _____

_____ _____ _____

These are growing patterns!

Complete each pattern.

_____

_____

_____

 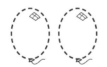

_____

What comes next? Circle your answer.

A	B	C	D	_____	
1	2	3	4	_____	5 6

Complete each pattern.

   _____ _____

   _____ _____

   _____ _____

   _____ _____

 _____ _____

 _____ _____ _____ _____

Great work! Bye!

222

COMPARING

Match the flowers. Color each pair the same.

Color in each box when you complete that page.

1 Introduction	2 Match the Same	3 Match & Color	4 Alike
5 Different	6 Figures & Shapes	7 Compare	8 Review

Draw lines!

Match the animals.

Color the things that are the same.

224

Color the objects.

= red   = blue   = yellow

Use the color code!

Match the fruit. Color each pair the same.

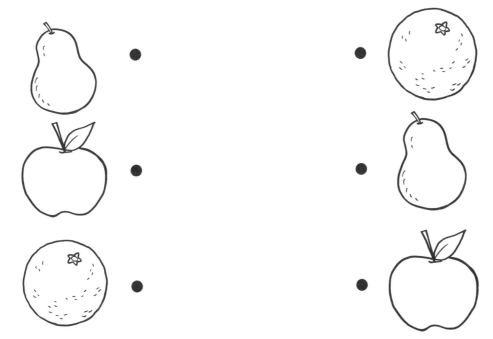

Alike means the same!

Color the things that are alike.

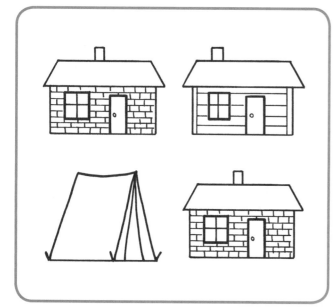 

Color the things that are the same.

Different means not the same!

Color each thing that is different.

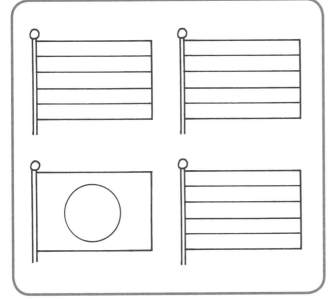

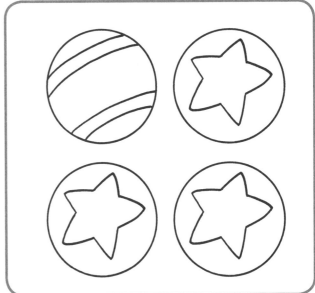

Color the thing in each row that is different.

Circle the figures that are the same as the first one.

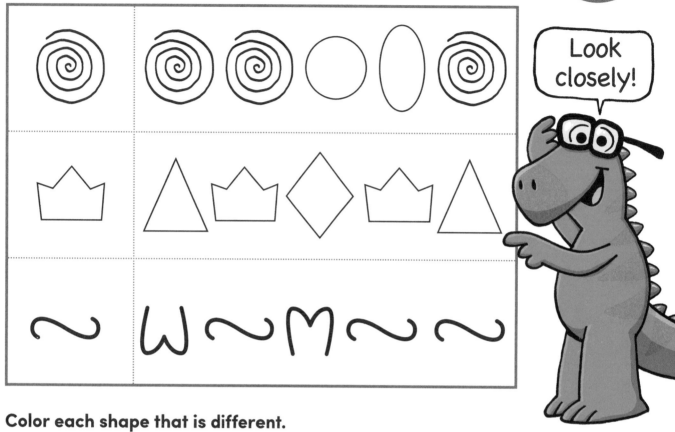

Look closely!

Color each shape that is different.

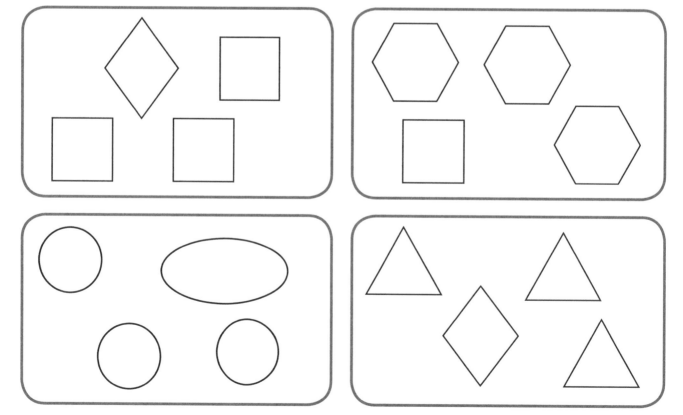

Look and compare!

Follow the directions for each box.

Color the short pencil.

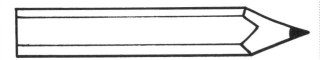

Color the long snake.

Color the big dog.

Color the little bird.

Color the tall tree.

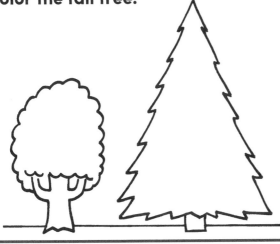

Color the short flower.

Circle the animals in each row that are the same.

Color the one that is different.

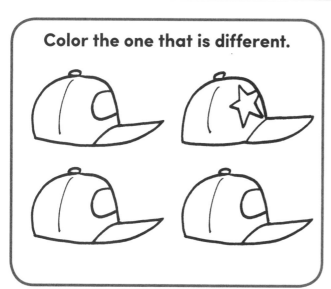

Color the one that is different.

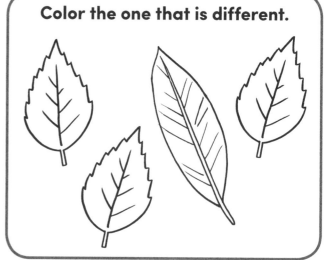

Color the long ties the same.

Color the short stools the same.

Great work! Bye!

CLASSIFYING

Color the things that belong together in each group.

Color in each box when you complete that page.

1	2	3	4
Introduction	Things That Do Not Belong	Food	Clothes
5	6	7	8
Animals	Things That Go Together	Attributes	Review

231

Circle the thing in each box that does not belong.

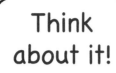 Think about it!

Color the things you can eat.

Find the food!

Circle the one that does not belong.

MILK

JUICE

Color the things you can wear.

Circle the one that does not belong.

Color the zoo animals.

Name the animals!

Circle the one that does not belong.

235

Match the things that go together.

Draw lines!

Circle the two things in each box that go together.

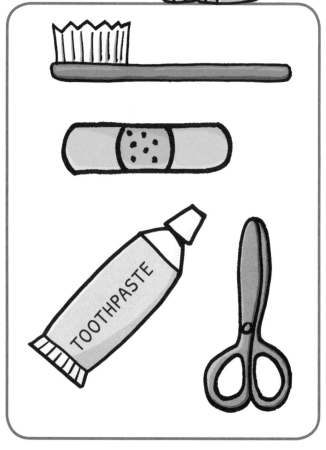

© Scholastic Inc.

Circle the things that are long.

Circle the things that are heavy.

© Scholastic Inc.

Match each picture to the group it belongs to.

 •

•

 •

•

 •

•

•

•

Circle each one that does not belong.

Great work!
Bye!

SEQUENCING

Draw the parts of the house in the correct order.

2 **1**

_Hi!_

Color in each box when you complete that page.

1	2	3	4
Introduction	Parts of a Picture	Before & After	Two-Part Sequences
5	6	7	8
Three-Part Sequences	Sequencing Words	Sequencing by Size	Review

Draw lines!

Put the parts of the pencil in order.

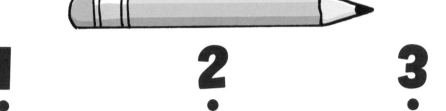

1

2

3

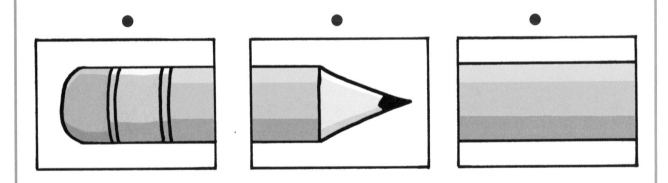

Now draw the parts of the pencil in the correct order.

Start by looking at the big picture!

Follow the directions for each box.

Circle what comes before.

Circle what comes after.

Circle what comes before.

Put the pictures in order.

Write 1 and 2!

Draw lines to show what happens first and last.

first

last

Write 1, 2, and 3!

Put the pictures in order.

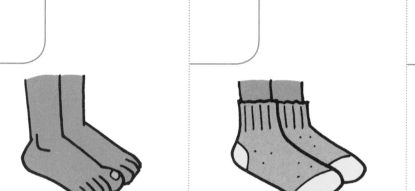

243

Put the pictures in order.

first

next

last

Put the objects in order from small to large.

Write 1, 2, and 3.

Put the objects in order from short to tall.

Draw the parts of the snake in the correct order.

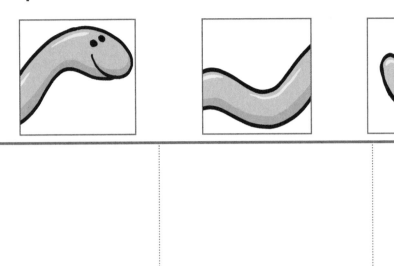

Circle what comes first.

Circle what comes last.

Put the pictures in order. Write 1, 2, and 3.

Great work! Bye!

Use the color code!

Trace and color each shape.

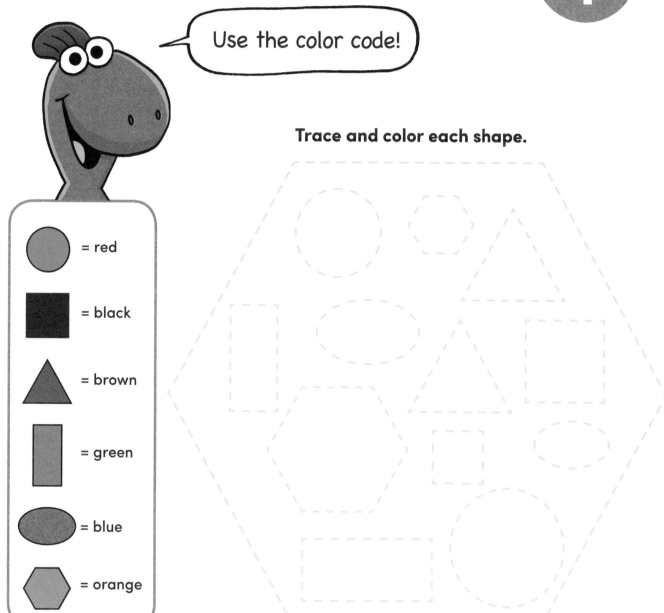

= red

= black

= brown

= green

= blue

= orange

Color in each box when you complete that page.

1	**2**	**3**	**4**
Colors & Shapes	Color Words	Shapes	Patterns
5	**6**	**7**	**8**
Same	Different	Classify	Sequencing

Say each color word!

Read the color words. Color the picture.

orange

black

yellow

red

red

yellow

purple

green

green

blue

white

white

orange

orange

white

purple

blue   blue

red

brown

green

yellow

purple

blue

purple

brown

brown

brown

248

Trace each path!

Help each rabbit get to its carrot.

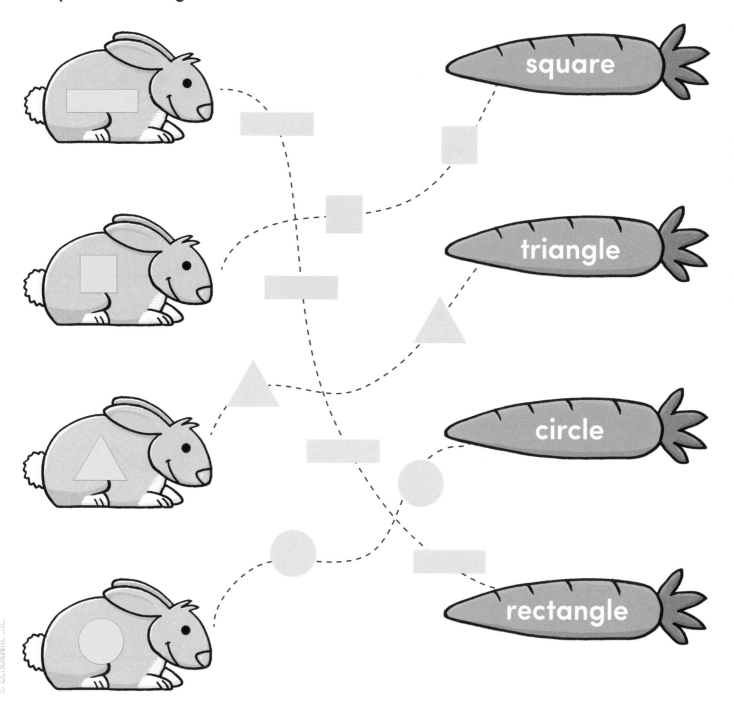

square

triangle

circle

rectangle

249

Match the patterns to help each bear find its banner.

Use these shapes:

Make your own pattern on the bear's banner.

Use the color code!

Find and color the twin animals.

Color the toy in each group that is different.

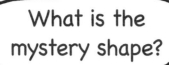

What is the mystery shape?

**Connect the dots from flower to flower.
Start at the arrow.**

Color each object that has the mystery shape.

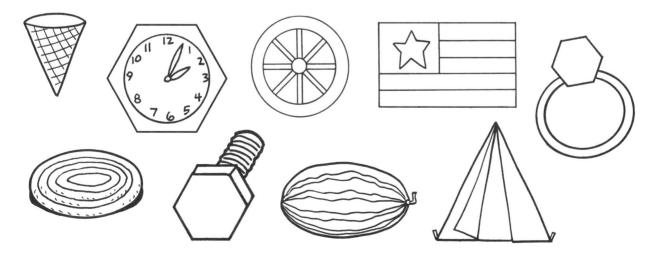

Help each kid put the cards in order. Write 1, 2, and 3.

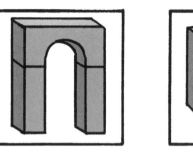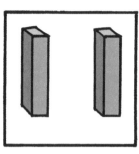

_____   _____   _____

_____   _____   _____

Draw the pictures in order to make a sun.

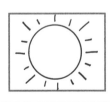

Great work! Bye!

254

CONGRATULATIONS!

This certificate is awarded to

FOR OUTSTANDING ACHIEVEMENT

Signed

Date

STK832316
PO# 5021789